THE NEGRO WORKER

STUDIES

IN LABOR

Consulting Editor,

HENRY DAVID

NATIONAL SCIENCE
FOUNDATION

The
NEGRO
WORKER

Ray Marshall

UNIVERSITY OF TEXAS

RANDOM HOUSE

New York

Preface

There can be little doubt that the race problem has been one of this country's most important domestic problems. The increasingly militant mood of the Negro community since the Second World War has given Negro employment problems a sense of urgency, for the achievement of civil rights will mean very little if the Negro is unable to secure the material means to translate these rights into concrete reality. It is equally clear, moreover, that the Negro's employment opportunities and conditions have important implications for the efficient use of human resources as well as for political, social, and economic stability. The parties to the employment relationship are confronted with the problem of resolving conflicting interests, because Negroes and their allies are challenging those institutions and arrangements that have for too long denied equal opportunities to Negro workers. It is hoped, of course, that these conflicts between Negroes, unions, management, and government agencies can be worked out by rules which will permit their peaceful resolution. This book is dedicated to the belief that the resolution of racial labor conflicts requires an understanding of the underlying factors influencing Negro employment conditions; my main purpose has been to seek this understanding.

The background for the development of Negro employment patterns is presented in Chapter I, which outlines the quantitative dimensions of Negro population and occupational patterns and discusses the influences of slavery, the Civil War, and Reconstruction on race and labor relations.

Chapter II examines the racial practices of the main national union federations in American labor history—the National Labor Union (NLU), the American Federation of Labor (AFL), and the Congress of Industrial Organizations (CIO). The relations between Negroes and the AFL-CIO, following the merger of the AFL and the CIO in 1956, are dealt with in Chapter III. These federations of local or national unions from the different trades or industries have become the broadest organizations in the American labor movement and therefore have had powers and objectives different from those held by national or local unions in particular crafts or industries. Thus, together, Chapters II and III attempt to account for the basic factors behind the evolution of relations between Negroes and the labor movement.

Although Negroes have had inadequate employment opportunities in all sections of the United States, racial employment patterns traditionally assumed their most rigid form in the South, where racial discrimination was formalized by law and custom. Chapter IV shows how the South's racial institutions have influenced unions in that region. Special emphasis is devoted to the impact of the racial ferment in the South during the 1950's and 1960's.

The main problems of racial discrimination within labor unions have been in the local and national unions; their practices are discussed in Chapter V. Before World War II, many national unions either excluded Negroes from membership by constitutional or other means or relegated Negro workers to inferior membership statuses in auxiliary locals controlled by whites. Unlike the auxiliaries, segregated locals were ostensibly autonomous organizations and were established by some national unions as a means of organizing Negro workers where local unions were restricted to whites. The most serious form of racial discrimination in 1966 was the exclusion of Negroes from membership in many local unions that controlled training and job opportunities. Although the responsibility for discrimination lies mainly with the local unions, the patterns of exclusion in some national organizations have been so complete as to suggest national policies. The national unions can also be accused of failing to use their power to eradicate discrimination on the part of their affiliated locals. Indeed, within the labor movement it can be argued that the national organizations have the main responsibility for eliminating discrimination, because as a general rule, only they have sufficient power to deal with this problem.

Chapter VI deals with recent trends in Negro income, employment, unemployment, labor force participation, and education and training. As is true throughout this volume, the main objective of Chapter VI is to discover underlying causal factors and to describe the patterns and changes produced by those factors. The chapter attempts to show that Negro employment problems are caused by a complex constellation of problems and not simply by discrimination.

A considerable body of public policy with respect to discrimination in employment has developed since 1940. The effectiveness of these laws and policies is discussed in Chapter VII. Special attention is devoted to government contract programs, state Fair Employment Practice (FEP) laws, court decisions, the National Labor Relations Act, the Railway Labor Act, and the Civil Rights Act of 1964. Chapter VIII speculates about trends in Negro-labor relations and Negro job opportunities.

The writer is indebted to many people and organizations for their help with this study. Much of the material used in this volume was collected in connection with various research projects, especially work for the Trade Union Project of the Fund for the Republic; a research project on labor in the South under the auspices of the Wertheim Committee, Harvard University; and a study of the impact of Federal policies on Negro employment in the South, undertaken on a Ford faculty research grant. I wish to thank John Wiley & Sons for permission to use material from my book *The Negro and Organized Labor* and the Industrial Relations Research Association for permission to use material taken from my paper "Negro Employment Opportunities: Problems and Prospects," published in the *Proceedings* of the Spring 1965 meeting. I am also indebted to Mrs. Miriam Z. Klipper and Mr. Henry David for their valuable editorial assistance.

Contents

THE NEGRO WORKER

Chapter I

THE NEGRO WORKER IN
EARLY AMERICA

The racial attitudes engendered by the American slave system have had a deep and continuing impact on labor race
relations. In the antebellum South, and to a lesser extent
in other areas of the country, direct and indirect competition between slaves and free workers created animosities
between black and white workers which lasted long after
emancipation. But the mutual antipathy between Negroes
and whites was not due entirely to competition for jobs.
It was based also on the fact that "The poor white envied
the slave's security and hated him for his material advantages, while the slave envied the white man's freedom
and hated him for the advantages of his whiteness." [1] Slavery also created the image of the Negro as an "inferior"
person and therefore influenced white attitudes about his
social, political, and economic acceptability. Although most
slaves and free Negroes lived in the South, the "race prob-

lem" created by the attitudes toward them has not been restricted to that region. Indeed, as the following discussion will show, the migration of Negroes out of the rural South has created many problems elsewhere.

Population Movements

In 1790, when the population of the United States was 3,172,006, the Negro population was 757,208. All but 59,527 of these Negroes were slaves; the rest were classified as "free colored persons." In 1840, when slaves constituted 15 percent of the population of the United States, the Southern states had the following proportions:

Virginia	36%	Tennessee	22%
North Carolina	33	Alabama	43
South Carolina	55	Mississippi	52
Georgia	41	Arkansas	20
Kentucky	23	Louisiana	48

SOURCE: *Compendium of the Enumeration of the Inhabitants and Statistics of the United States as Obtained at the Department of State from the Returns of the Sixth Census.* "Tables of Apportionment," p. 364.

Outside the South, no state had a slave population large enough to be recorded in the 1840 census except Delaware (3 percent), Maryland (19 percent), and Missouri (15 percent).

Table 1.1 shows, by region, the population distribution in 1860. The nearly 4 million slaves in the South in 1860 were owned by families that represented only 1.75 million of the region's more than 7 million whites.

TABLE 1.1

REGION	WHITE	FREE NEGRO	SLAVE
South	7,033,973	258,000	3,838,765
Northeast	10,438,028	155,983	18
North Central	8,899,969	69,291	114,948
West	550,567	4,450	29

SOURCE: *Department of Commerce, Bureau of the Census. Historical Statistics of the United States, 1789–1945,* 1949, p. 25.

Although most Negroes remained in the South until the 1960's, the tendency for them to migrate to other areas started immediately after the Civil War and was stimulated by World War II. Of 7,450,589 nonwhites in the United States in 1890, 6,915,715 were born in the South, and of that number only 526,612, or 7.6 percent, lived outside that region. The proportion of nonwhites born in the South and living in other regions was only 4.2 percent in 1900, but jumped to 8.1 percent in 1920, when 9,676,149 of the nation's 10,623,838 nonwhites were born in the South. In 1860, 5.1 percent of all Negroes lived outside the South, where they constituted 1.2 percent of the total population, but by 1910 10.4 percent of the Negroes lived outside the South, where they made up 1.6 percent of the population. The census figures for the proportion of nonwhites in the South after 1910 were:

1920	85%
1930	74
1940	74
1950	64
1960	57

The 1960 figure of 57 percent really overstates the proportion of nonwhites in the South because it is based on the census definition of the South, which includes Maryland, the District of Columbia, and Delaware, and shows a total of 1,098,146 nonwhites. If we subtract these three areas the remaining states, the states of the Southeast and Southwest, contained only 10,400,000 of the 20,500,000 nonwhites in the United States. The "South" as defined in this more restricted sense had the following proportions of the nonwhite population:

1940	73%
1950	60
1960	51

Why the decreasing percentage? Although the factors responsible for the patterns of Negro migration are not completely known, some of the more important causes seem reasonably clear. The increased migration of Negroes to Northern areas around 1915 undoubtedly was caused by a combination of factors including: industrial expansion in the North, which increased the demand for unskilled labor; labor shortages resulting from the cessation of immigration during World War I; the lure of freedom and greater opportunities in the North as compared with the South; and the worsening of conditions in Southern agriculture due to the boll weevil, drought, soil depletion, and high birth rates.

The main trend in the shift of Negro population has been to the cities, and out of the South and into the Northeast and Midwest. Before World War II, very few Negroes lived in the West; as late as 1940 only 2.2 percent of the Negroes in the United States lived in Western states. In the North, Negroes migrated primarily to such cities as New York, Chicago, Philadelphia, Detroit, Cleveland, and Pittsburgh, which had about a third of the Northern Negro population in 1930 and about half of that population in 1940.

Most Northern Negroes have lived in cities and, although there has been an urban trend in the South, most Southern Negroes lived in rural areas until before World War II. About 64 percent of Northern Negroes lived in cities in 1860 as compared with 79 percent in 1910. Only 6.7 percent of Southern Negroes lived in urban areas in 1860, but this figure had increased to 22 percent by 1910. Negroes constituted 19.3 percent of the Southern urban population in 1860 and 24.5 percent in 1910. In 1960, 35 percent of American Negroes lived in Southern urban areas and 38 percent lived in Northern urban areas; only about a fourth of the nation's Negroes remained in Southern rural areas.

Not only were over three-quarters of all American Negroes still in the South on the eve of World War II, but Negroes were still concentrated primarily in the same areas as in 1860, namely the so-called "Black Belt" that forms a crescent of counties from the Potomac to Texas. Part of the explanation for the surprising continuity in the location of Negroes was the segregated occupational system which tended to restrict Negroes to agriculture and to only certain kinds of nonagricultural occupations. It is particularly significant that Negroes did not participate to an appreciable degree in the "New South's" nonagricultural industries, which grew up after the Civil War mainly outside the "Black Belt."

The Negro Work Force

Although most slaves were employed in agriculture, they also were trained for a variety of nonagricultural trades, especially those connected with the building crafts. Plantation owners frequently apprenticed their slaves to journeymen for training, and sometimes traveling teachers instructed them in various crafts. Planters rented their trained slaves to others during slack seasons on the home plantation, and white journeymen often augmented their incomes and supported themselves in retirement by buying and training slaves.[2]

Slaves were also used to frustrate the free workers' efforts to organize. In 1846, for instance, the superintendent of a South Carolina canal and railroad company recommended to his board of directors that slaves be bought to head off strikes, and other employers argued that a supply of slave mechanics was "our bulwark against extortion and our safeguard against the turbulence of white mechanics, as seen in the great strikes, both in England and in the North, and is the only protection we have in any possible struggle between capital and white labor."[3] The famed Tredegar Iron Company of Richmond used free labor almost exclusively until the 1840's, but in 1842 the company started employing slaves as a means of reducing labor costs. In 1847, when their white workers struck for higher wages and the removal of Negro workers, Tredegar broke the strike by expanding the use of slaves and by threatening to prosecute the strikers for criminal conspiracy. After the strike,[4] the company gradually filled almost all nonsupervisory jobs with slaves.

Pressure felt by white labor due to the presence of Negro workers was not restricted to the South. Spero and Harris tell us, "In the North, the presence of the free Negro workman was resented even more sharply than in the South." [5] It was even illegal for free Negroes to live in several Northern states and municipalities. In 1834, for example, a New Jersey newspaper called for the "rigid enforcement of the statute against the admission of blacks into our boundaries," when Negroes fleeing from a mob in Philadelphia sought refuge in that state.[6] Negroes had predominated in Philadelphia's nonagricultural work force before 1834, but subsequently were replaced by immigrants. White workers seriously objected to Negro competition in Cincinnati and New York, and in smaller cities in Illinois, Indiana, New Jersey, and Pennsylvania. Indeed, opposition to Negroes was so great that the Democratic party of New York City actually opposed the freeing of slaves for fear that it would lead to an influx of hordes of Negro workers from the South.

In spite of opposition from whites, Negroes were trained for many nonagricultural jobs before the Civil War; they seem to have predominated in many skilled crafts. Skilled immigrants, who made up an important part of the labor force of Northern cities, avoided the South. Although we have no good statistical evidence for the occupational distribution of Negroes before the Civil War, a survey made under the auspices of the Federal Government in 1865 indicates that Negroes constituted 80 percent of the South's skilled mechanics at that time, a proportion undoubtedly influenced by the fact that many white artisans had been drawn away by the war.[7]

Due to a variety of factors, the Negro's position in the Southern labor force changed markedly after 1865. The main occupations open to Negroes after Reconstruction were those which were regarded as "Negro" jobs (which were, by definition, hot, dirty, or otherwise disagreeable), those for which they were trained as slaves, or occupations which served the Negro communities. Racial job patterns had a strong caste element about them. Slavery and color marked the Negro as an inferior person; therefore whites considered it improper for Negroes to compete directly with them for the better jobs. It was especially unthinkable that Negroes should hold supervisory positions over whites.

Negro workers were to be found especially in the following industries: fertilizer, cigar and tobacco, slaughter and packing, lumber and furniture, turpentine and distillery, road and bridge construction and repair, steam railroad, water transportation, hotel and restaurant, laundry and cleaning, and dyeing and pressing.

Although, following the Civil War, Negroes were in many ways better off in the North than in the South they had better opportunities in the South in some professions and in some skilled trades. Frazier tells us that except where he had broken in as a strikebreaker, the Negro in the North was confined principally to domestic and personal service occupations.[8] After a careful study of conditions North and South, Myrdal concluded in 1944:

> Except during the war boom, Negroes realized that there were only a limited number of jobs in the North. Owners of Northern industry were not very willing to hire Negro workers except when orders were piling up, and European immigrant laborers could not be had because of the War or legal restrictions on immigration. Northern industrialists often believed in the stereotype of the lazy and inefficient Negro, and often their limited observations strengthened their belief. Some had the legitimate doubt whether Negroes, used to forced labor on farms, could be adapted to free labor in factories. Too, they did not wish to offend their white workers, who were in the majority. Most white unions, faced with Negroes coming into their industries, fought the Negroes; and white workers generally opposed black competition.[9]

The overall statistics on Negro employment in the South and the non-South indicate that racial employment patterns were only slightly more favorable to Negroes in the non-South. Table 1.2 shows the distribution of male employment in 1930.

TABLE 1.2

OCCUPATION GROUP	SOUTH		NON-SOUTH	
	NEGRO	WHITE	NEGRO	WHITE
Total	100%	100%	100%	100%
Clerical or lower	95	79	95	82
Skilled or lower	93	60	91	64
Semiskilled or lower	86	38	83	41
Unskilled	71	20	66	21

SOURCE: *Socio-Economic Grouping of the Gainful Workers of the United States, 1930* (Washington, D.C.: Bureau of the Census, 1938), p. 36.

About 69 percent of nonwhite women were employed in domestic and personal services in 1940 and 60 percent remained in these occupation groups in 1962. About 41 percent of nonwhite males were farm workers in 1940 as compared with 14 percent in 1962.

The percentages of Negroes in some of the main building trades for various census years are shown in Table 1.3.

TABLE 1.3

CRAFT	1940	1930	1920	1910	1900	1890
Bricklayers	6.0%	6.9%	8.1%	7.5%	9.0%	6.1%
Carpenters	3.9	3.5	3.9	4.3	3.7	3.6
Cement finishers	15.2	15.8	15.4	13.0	10.5	10.3
Electricians	.7	.7	.6	.6	—	—
Painters	3.8	3.6	3.2	2.9	2.1	2.0
Plumbers	2.2	2.0	1.7	1.7	1.2	1.1

The Entrenchment of Segregation

Thus, emancipation and Reconstruction did very little to improve the economic condition of Negroes, in spite of high initial hopes and expectations. After the dream that the Yankee would furnish him forty acres and a mule had faded, the freedman was forced to turn to his old master and to the sharecropping system for subsistence. The low rate of economic growth in the South before 1880 made it difficult for Negroes to move into urban occupations, and Negroes thus tended to become frozen to agriculture. But even when he did move to town, the Negro was usually excluded from most of the new nonagricultural occupations except for disagreeable or low status "Negro" jobs. Except where the number of Negroes made it impossible, most unions either excluded or segregated Negroes. The main exceptions were the trowel trade unions, which had many Negro members, and the abortive attempts to form equalitarian unions made by the National Labor Union and the Knights of Labor, discussed in the following chapter. Moreover, there were no longer slaveowners who could use their power to protect Negroes from the hostility of white workers. Indeed, the planters now took measures to restrict the Negro's movements in order to assure a continuous supply of labor for the plantations. These restrictive measures included the so-called "Black Codes," which were ostensibly vagrancy laws, and the use of a credit system which prevented Negroes from leaving the plantations until they cleared their debts with the planter.

Whites as well as Negroes suffered from the depressed condition of the Southern economy in the years following the Civil War. Because of credit shortages and the commercialization of agriculture, many planters were forced to leave the plantations or to remain as masters of declining estates. Poor whites and Negroes alike suffered from high birth rates, ignorance, depletion of the soil, high interest rates, and the disadvantages of the sharecropping system. However, although white sharecroppers were given no better employment terms than their Negro competitors after 1910 when segregation became firmly entrenched, they had greater freedom to move into nonagricultural jobs for which they could qualify, they had the right to vote, and they benefited from whatever comfort they derived from feelings of racial superiority.

These advantages were often more apparent than real, however, because it was very difficult for most Southern whites to overcome their environment and acquire good nonagricultural jobs. Moreover, white supremacy attitudes did harm in other areas, for the dominance of the race issue in Southern politics imposed a false unity of whites and prevented effective political solutions to many of the region's pressing economic problems. The South has defended its racial policies, which originated in the defense of slavery and were strengthened by the Civil War and Reconstruction, as necessary in order to keep the Negro from "taking over" as he is presumed to have done during Reconstruction, even though not many Negroes were elected to office at that time.[10]

This solid political tradition was not established immediately. For some time after 1877, following the withdrawal of Federal troops from the South, the Negro vote was coveted by conservatives and liberals alike. According to C. Vann Woodward, during the 1880's Southern Democrats and Republicans competed vigorously for the Negro vote. "The Negro voters were therefore courted, 'mistered,' and honored by Southern white politicians as never before." [11] It even appeared for a time that Southern Negroes and whites might be welded together politically and economically in such equalitarian labor federations as the National Labor Union, the Knights of Labor, and the Populist movement of the 1880's and 1890's. Ironically, however, the Populists were defeated by Negro votes that were controlled by conservative Democrats in the plantation belts. The Populists therefore became convinced that an economically oriented political movement required the disfranchisement of Negroes. Of course, many whites also favored disfranchisement because they feared that Negroes would become the balance of political power if whites split along economic lines. But once the Negro was in effect disfranchised through white primaries, poll taxes, and other restrictions, demagogues were able for many years to use the race issue to defeat the Republican party and to prevent Negroes from becoming significant politically. We shall see that the Knights of Labor and the National Labor Union were also unable to overcome racial policy differences in their ranks.

Just as the disfranchisement of Negroes did not occur immediately after the withdrawal of Federal troops, the rigid form of legal racial segregation which became the pattern in the South took some time to develop. Whether from fear of a return of Yankee troops or recognition of the importance of the Negro vote, it was about a decade after the end of military occupation before the first segregation laws were passed.[12] By 1900, however, complete segregation became the accepted way of handling the race problem. A belief that most Northerners favored segregation and therefore would not send the troops back emboldened the South in this course. This conviction was supported by the segregation of the Negro in the Federal army; the prevalence of segregation in the North; the acquiescence of Northerners in the political compromise of 1877, which resulted in the withdrawal of Federal troops; and, finally, a series of United States Supreme Court decisions between 1873 and 1898 that established the legality of "separate but equal facilities" and denied the Negro Federal protection for acts committed against him by private individuals.

By 1900, therefore, Southern Negroes had become almost completely segregated by either law or custom. They rode in separate compartments or in the back of public conveyances, went to segregated public schools, could not marry whites, were buried in segregated cemeteries, and ate in separate restaurants. Employment, as we have seen, was also segregated. In the North, where unions were stronger and where there were fewer Negro craftsmen, resistance to Negroes was so strong that Negro leaders advised Negro workers to return to the South where the skilled crafts were still open to them.[13] In 1905, John R. Commons concluded that the Plasterers, Carpenters, Masons, and Painters admitted Negroes freely in the South, but that few Northern plasterers' unions and almost none of the other crafts accepted Negroes.[14] These relationships, between unions and the Negro community, are explored further in the following chapter.

Chapter II

NATIONAL LABOR FEDERATIONS AND THE NEGRO, 1866–1956

As was demonstrated in Chapter I, slavery, the Civil War, emancipation, and Reconstruction had important consequences for labor race relations. Because the freeing of some 4 million slaves greatly increased the free labor force of the South, that region obviously had the most important and immediate problems of racial accommodation. These problems became more national in scope after the 1880's, when industrialization brought nonunion Southern employers into closer competition with firms in the rest of the country and gave Northern unions a strong motive to extend their influence into the South. Industrialization was also accompanied by an increasing migration of Negroes out of the rural South. It therefore became necessary for labor organizations to reconcile the racial attitudes of many different groups. This chapter examines the ways in which national labor federations reconciled these pressures in the years before the 1956 merger of the AFL-CIO.

These national federations, comprising various geographical subordinates, local unions, and national trade unions, are the broadest labor organizations in the United States. Although there were some earlier city federations, the first national trades organization was the short-lived National Trades Union of 1834; it was followed by the National Labor Union (NLU).

The National Labor Union, formed in 1866, was the first labor federation after the Civil War. The NLU attempted to follow an equalitarian racial policy from the outset. At its first convention it urged all unions to make "no distinction of race or nationality," [1] arguing that Negroes were going to be trained for a variety of occupations and therefore the interests of all workers required that they be organized. It was not, however, possible for the NLU to implement this policy at the local level, for some of its affiliates refused to organize Negro workers. In addition, the political differences between Negroes and whites made it difficult for them to cooperate—the NLU's leaders generally backed Democratic programs at a time when most Negro leaders were Republicans.

In 1869, the Knights of Labor was formed, stressing the formation of workers' cooperatives and advocating educational and political programs for solving the problems of the capitalist system. Its members were organized into trade assemblies of workers in a given trade or mixed assemblies of workers from diverse trades. Five local assemblies could form a district assembly. T. V. Powderly, the Knights' Grand Master Workman, once declared that the Knights of Labor would accept all men who worked for a living, but "no drones, no lawyers, no bankers, no doctors, no professional politicians." [2] The Knights therefore accepted all workers without regard to race, creed, color, or national origin. At its peak in 1886, the Knights had perhaps 60,000 Negroes in a total membership of over 700,000. Negroes attended the Knights' conventions and apparently were courteously received. Indeed, the KL gained considerable publicity in 1886, when the majority of its delegates to the Richmond Convention withdrew from a hotel which would not permit a Negro delegate to be seated. Like the NLU, however, the Knights could not always implement their equalitarian policies at the local level and, conceding to the customs of the time, they organized segregated locals in the South.[3] Moreover, then, as now, it was easier for a politically oriented federation to make equalitarian pronouncements than it was for local collective bargaining organizations to enforce those policies.

The American Federation of Labor

The main labor federation in American labor history before the 1930's was the American Federation of Labor (AFL), organized in 1886. From its inception, Samuel Gompers and other AFL leaders were committed to organizing workers without regard to race or religion. This policy seems to have been steadfastly followed until about 1895, when the Machinists were admitted to the federation by the subterfuge of transferring the race bar in their constitution to their ritual.[4] The Machinists were admitted to the AFL in the only year that Samuel Gompers was defeated for the presidency between the time the federation was formed and his death in 1924. Gompers had attempted to get the Machinists to abolish their discriminatory policies, and failing that, recommended the formation of a rival labor organization, The International Machinists' Union. However, this recommendation was rejected by a special study committee, probably for fear of dual unionism; union leaders have always been afraid that dual unionism would destroy the labor movement.

Ideologically, the AFL never abandoned its opposition to excluding Negroes from its affiliated unions, but Gompers apparently surrendered to the reality of racial discrimination among the federation's locals. While he continued to emphasize that the better part of economic good sense was to organize workers regardless of race, creed, or color, he finally decided that it was better to organize whites and Negroes into segregated locals than not to organize them at all. Both the AFL and Gompers chose to believe that it would be easier to reform discriminatory unions *after* they were admitted to the federation and that to keep them out would weaken the trade union movement. In point of fact, the AFL Executive Council was virtually powerless to force its affiliates to comply with its expressed democratic principles, for the federation was a voluntary organization whose main weapon was moral pressure. Once the AFL admitted the Machinists, it could hardly refuse to accept other unions which discriminated against Negroes.

When the Order of Railway Telegraphers and the Brotherhood of Railway Trackmen were admitted to the federation in 1899—four years after the Machinists— Gompers apparently did not protest their anti-Negro rules. A year later, the federation adopted the policy of giving AFL charters to Negro locals and central labor unions where, in the judgment of the Executive Council, "it [appeared] advisable and in the best interests of the trade union movement to do so." [5] After 1900, the federation admitted many unions whose constitutions barred Negroes from membership and permitted some affiliates to change their constitutions to accomplish this objective.

As noted in Chapter I, many factors contributed to the rigid pattern of segregation which emerged in the South by 1900. Trade unionism merely reflected and reinforced community practices. The attitudes of white workers, supported by powerful social pressures from the white community, could have enforced job segregation, whether or not they were aided by union discrimination. Economic hardships, that limited economic opportunities for all workers, reinforced the white community's desire to restrict the better jobs to whites.

In view of these circumstances, it was perhaps natural for Negro leaders to ally themselves with powerful employers, especially with some big companies and those with headquarters outside the South who were willing to work with Negro leaders like Booker T. Washington in order to get a steady supply of cheap nonunion labor. In his famous Atlanta Exposition address of 1895, Washington advised Negroes to shun politics and to acquire the necessary skills to meet the competition of whites. And in an article that appeared in the *Atlantic Monthly* Washington explained the pro-employer sentiments of Negroes as follows:

> The average Negro who comes to town does not understand the necessity or advantage of a labor organization which stands between him and his employer and aims apparently to make a monopoly of the opportunity for labor. . . . [He is] more accustomed to work for persons than for wages. When he gets a job, therefore, he is inclined to consider the source from which it comes.[6]

Antiunionism among Negroes even extended to unions that admitted them. And though the extent to which Negroes were used as strikebreakers probably has been exaggerated, Negroes did play an important role before the 1930's in breaking strikes in such industries as meatpacking, steel, coal and ore mining, automobiles, and railroads. White workers were also extensively employed to break strikes in these industries, but Negroes were far more conspicuous and far more resented by the strikers.[7]

It is clear that Negro-AFL relations were, to say the least, strained by World War I. It is equally clear that both Negroes and union leaders considered the other side to be at fault. This is evident in the following statement by Gompers to a group of Negro leaders who came to discuss this problem with the AFL Executive Council in 1917.

> In many instances the conduct of colored workmen, and those who have spoken for them, has not been in asking or demanding that equal rights be accorded to them as to white workmen, but somehow conveying the idea that they are to be petted or coddled and given special consideration and special privilege. Of course that can't be done.[8]

For good measure, he added, with respect to Washington, "we could not get [from him] anything like an expression of hearty accord with our movement." [9] Gompers justified the discriminatory policies of the AFL and its affiliates on the grounds that their first duty was to unionize workers.

In summary, Gompers at first believed that he could at least be an influence toward equalitarian union racial policies by withholding affiliation from those who failed to follow the federation's egalitarian credo. But the pressures from some of its affiliates and applicants for affiliation forced the AFL to admit unions that excluded Negroes. Pro-employer and antiunion attitudes of influential Negro leaders encouraged Negroes to act as strikebreakers, which further weakened the ability of the federation to restrain racist white union leadership. Although many of the AFL's autonomous affiliated unions also practiced the most blatant forms of discrimination, the federation itself did not surrender egalitarianism as its official ideology. This official ideology, while it may have seemed hollow to Negroes, nevertheless eventually made it possible for Negro trade union leaders to press for elimination of discrimination within the trade union movement.

Union racial practices have been formed, perpetuated, and changed by a complex constellation of dynamic social, economic, and political forces. Industrialization, urbanization, and Negro migrations probably were the most important factors tending to change race relations in unions as well as in society as a whole. The industrialization of the United States, and of the South after the 1880's, caused many Northern employers to look to the South for a source of cheap manpower to man the mines, factories, and steel mills. The steady flow of Negroes out of the rural South was stimulated by wars and other events. Wars not only increased the demand for labor, but, by halting immigration from abroad, reduced the available supply of unskilled white labor. The demand for Negro labor continued during the 1920's as employers turned to Negro strikebreakers to buttress their antiunion "open shop" movements and as Congressional action permanently diminished the flow of immigrants into this country. These developments wrought a virtual transformation of the Negro population. In contrast to only 12 percent in 1910 and 26 percent in 1930, by 1964 over half of all American Negroes lived outside the states that had made up the Confederacy, and 90 percent of employed Negroes worked outside of agriculture.[10]

The urbanization of the Negro population had important consequences for race relations. In the first place, it increased the Negroes' political power, especially in the North, where Negroes had the right to vote. The urban environment also tended to raise the Negroes' aspirations and caused them to make greater demands for equal education, civil rights, and job opportunities.

Migration also brought the Negro increasingly into conflict with white workers and their unions. Race riots erupted in the North as employers imported Negroes as strikebreakers, or as cheap labor, or in an effort to avert the unionization of their companies. There were particularly bitter race riots in East St. Louis and Chicago, Illinois, in 1917 and 1919.[11] The expansion of union membership during World War I brought the unions face to face with the Negro problem. Some unions responded by organizing Negroes on an equal basis with whites, but, where they would not, the AFL followed its policy of chartering locals which were affiliated directly with the federation. This policy proved quite unsatisfactory, however, because the AFL usually followed the interests of international unions and did not adequately represent the Negroes in these federal locals. The Negro federal locals in jurisdictions covered by discriminating railroad unions asked the AFL either to require these discriminating unions to admit Negroes or to grant the federal locals a national charter. These demands went unheeded, however, as the international unions responded by organizing Negroes into so-called auxiliary locals, an arrrangement that was bitterly opposed by Negroes, who were thus denied equal representation. Although some Negroes remained in the auxiliaries as a condition for retaining their jobs, others rejected this inferior status and refused to join the unions. The auxiliaries also proved unsatisfactory to the unions because they could neither present a united front in collective bargaining nor collect dues from Negroes in their jurisdictions who, in spite of their unequal status, often benefited from the unions' collective bargaining activities.

Another factor tending to change the racial practices of the AFL and its affiliates was the growth of organized Negro opposition to union discrimination. Two of these organizations, the National Association for the Advancement of Colored People (NAACP) and the National Urban League (NUL), frequently called upon the AFL to eradicate racial discrimination.

There were also a number of Negro labor organizations which sought to fight discrimination from within the labor movement. By far the most important of these organizations was the Brotherhood of Sleeping Car Porters (BSCP), which had an influence in the Negro community and in the labor movement far out of proportion to its size. The leader of the BSCP, A. Philip Randolph, has for over forty years been the symbol of the Negro fighting for recognition within the trade unions. The BSCP was organized in 1925 and, after a decade of jurisdictional conflicts with various AFL unions, was chartered as a national union by the AFL in 1936. The BSCP received its national charter despite the bitter protests of several national unions, and the Negro labor organization's case was strengthened in 1935 when it won a National Mediation Board election and acquired sole bargaining rights for the porters.

After its admission to the AFL, the BSCP waged a constant attack against the AFL and its affiliates in an effort to get them to abolish discrimination. At first, delegates to the AFL conventions paid little attention to attacks from Randolph, Milton Webster, and other BSCP leaders. Indeed, AFL delegates would either walk out or mill around talking while Randolph delivered his verbal blasts. Undeterred by this treatment, Randolph and his colleagues continued the attacks; they became increasingly effective as their charges received greater publicity and as the race question became an increasingly grave threat to the AFL. Indeed, at the 1941 convention, Randolph forced top AFL officials into an extensive debate on union racial discrimination. By that time, growing competition between the AFL and the Congress of Industrial Organizations (CIO) had increased the AFL leaders' sensitivity to Randolph's charges. Legislation passed during the 1930's to encourage collective bargaining where workers voted for union representation caused unions to relax their discriminatory policies in order to compete for the Negro vote. And, as we shall see, the Negro vote often was decisive.

By the time of the formation of the CIO, a number of pressures were being exerted on the AFL to cause it to change its racial practices. While the AFL's policies must be distinguished from those of its affiliates, it is important to note that the federation itself issued charters to directly affiliated, segregated central bodies and local unions and failed to protect adequately the Negroes' interests in these organizations. After about 1939, however, the AFL seems to have discontinued the practice of giving charters to racially segregated central labor organizations.[12] The forces tending to undermine discrimination by unions included continued movement of Negroes into jobs over which unions had jurisdiction; pressure from within the AFL from the BSCP and other Negro organizations; external pressures from the growing Negro communities in the North; and, perhaps most important, competition between unions for Negro membership. The last point became especially important with the upsurge of union membership associated with the New Deal and with the formation of the CIO.

The Congress of Industrial Organizations

As a result of what its leaders thought was the AFL's failure to take full advantage of the favorable organizing climate of the 1930's, in 1935, the CIO was formed; it was subsequently expelled from the AFL for dual unionism. At the same time, the Wagner Act was passed, greatly strengthening prospects for the organizing of unions by giving workers the right to vote for their own bargaining representatives, by outlawing certain unfair labor practices used by employers to defeat unions, and by creating a National Labor Relations Board (NLRB) with the power to enforce the law. The AFL responded to the CIO's challenge by extending its membership in older jurisdictions and by launching organizing drives in new fields. It was this rivalry that caused the AFL and its affiliates to relax some of their racial restrictions. The CIO adopted an equalitarian racial position from the beginning. One reason for this position was the CIO's desire to appeal to the large numbers of Negroes in the steel, auto, mining, packing, rubber, and other mass production industries. No CIO leader better understood the importance of equalitarian racial policies for successful unionism than John L. Lewis of the United Mine Workers, who provided much of the financial and leadership support for the CIO.[13] The UMW had long had a favorable reputation among Negroes in both the North and the South because of its steadfast refusal to sanction discrimination, even in the face of vigorous opposition in the important Southern coal areas.

The CIO's equalitarian racial policies stemmed directly from the ideological positions held by many of its leaders, who were young, idealistic people with broad social outlooks. Some of them were Communists, a group which has almost always adopted equalitarian racial positions. Although many doubted the sincerity of the Communists' racial policies, there can be little question that, by emphasizing the race issue to get Negro support, the Communists forced white union leaders into paying more attention to racial matters.

The CIO's racial policies were also influenced by its industrial structure, which gave its leaders a much different outlook from that of the craft-oriented leaders of the AFL. Industrial unions have very little control over the racial composition of their membership because they do not control jobs; they attempt to organize workers who are already employed. Craft unions, on the other hand, have the ability to determine whom the employer hires because they often control the supply of labor. In one of the main differences between craft and industrial unions, therefore, lies the opportunity for discrimination; the industrial union has less opportunity for discrimination. Moreover, the industrial union structure, and the fact that many of its unions were organized from the top down, gave the CIO more power to enforce its policies.

The age of a labor organization also tends to influence its racial policies, although many other forces are at work. In race relations, as in other matters, unions tend to reflect their environment. Therefore, a union which was formed in the 1890's, when segregation was becoming institutionalized, would be much more likely to adopt a segregationist position than an organization such as the CIO that was formed during the 1930's.

Finally, a union's racial practices tend to be conditioned by its objectives and the importance of Negroes in the attainment of those objectives. A narrow, job-oriented organization is likely to discriminate against Negroes or other groups if its leaders feel that discrimination strengthens the economic position of the members. On the other hand, an organization like the CIO, which has broad social objectives, would appeal to the Negro community for political support in helping to achieve those objectives.

These several considerations help explain why the CIO adopted a nondiscrimination policy and made vigorous efforts to gain a favorable image among Negroes. These efforts included financial contributions to organizations such as the NAACP and to Negro churches and newspapers, the adoption of equalitarian racial resolutions, the use of Negroes to organize in Negro communities, the creation of the Committee to Abolish Racial Discrimination as an organization to help implement its nondiscrimination policy, and the service of its leaders in official positions in such organizations as the National Association for the Advancement of Colored People and the National Urban League. Although the NAACP and the NUL had been very skeptical of the sincerity of the AFL's claims to an equalitarian position even during the 1930's, they were convinced of the genuineness of the CIO's policies and urged Negroes to join that organization. This position did not go unopposed within these organizations, however, because some of the pro-employer Negro leaders strongly objected to Negroes joining unions. But the potential power of the CIO and the programs of the New Deal designed to help Negroes greatly reduced the influence of antiunion and Republican Negro leaders.

The cooperative relationship between the CIO and the Negro community proved mutually beneficial. The NAACP actively campaigned for CIO unions and Walter White, NAACP executive secretary, personally aided the United Automobile Workers in their drive to organize the Ford Motor Company.[14] For their part, the unions gave financial support to Negro organizations, and CIO presidents Philip Murray and Walter Reuther served as members of the NAACP Board of Directors. Unions also gave significant legislative and organizational support to civil rights legislation, prompting Thurgood Marshall, the NAACP's chief legal adviser, to declare that "the program of the CIO has become a Bill of Rights for Negro labor in America." [15]

Although the CIO succeeded in gaining a favorable image in the Negro community, it would be misleading to leave the impression that the CIO automatically followed equalitarian policies and received Negro support while all AFL locals discriminated and were shunned by Negroes. Some CIO locals barred Negroes from membership and others permitted segregated locals; and Negroes either segregated themselves, or were segregated by whites, in many —and perhaps most—of the "integrated" CIO unions in the South. Indeed, CIO President Philip Murray was infuriated when, shortly before his death in 1952, he addressed an audience of the Steelworkers (of which he was the national president) in Alabama that was segregated; when the crowd spilled out of the union hall into the street, local union officials gave policemen orders to maintain segregation in the street. As late as 1964, there were segregated facilities in local union headquarters of the Steelworkers in Birmingham.

But the most serious problem for Negroes in CIO unions was the restriction of Negroes to certain jobs. These seniority arrangements were not entirely the responsibility of the unions, of course, but few CIO unions actively tried to abolish segregated seniority rosters in the South. Nor was this problem restricted to the South, for CIO members struck throughout the United States during World War II when Negroes were hired or upgraded into formerly all-white organizations. For example, in December 1944, over 1,000 white employees at the Pullman Standard Car Manufacturing Company in Chicago struck to prevent the promotion to gang leader of a Negro pipefitter. Both management and the United Steelworkers' leadership opposed this strike. Another Steelworkers' plant was struck in East St. Louis, Illinois, when a Negro was promoted to crane operator. The union again backed the Negro and the strike was broken. In 1944, at Harvey, Illinois, 300 white workers struck for four days for segregated toilets. In Cincinnati, Ohio, 15,000 white workers represented by the UAW struck to prevent the promotion of 7 Negroes. The UAW supported the company and the strike was broken. The UAW had to put down a number of strikes by its white members in Detroit against the hiring and upgrading of Negroes during World War II. (Cases in the files of the CIO Civil Rights Committee.) It should be noted, however, that the CIO's national affiliates almost invariably cooperated with employers in putting down these racial strikes and there appears to have been considerable upgrading of Negroes outside the South during World War II.

In longshoring and the building trades, where, in the South, the AFL had many more Negro members than the CIO, the CIO was unable to shake the loyalty of the Negro workers to the AFL, even though Negroes were usually restricted to segregated locals. Indeed, in some cases the AFL even won bargaining rights away from CIO unions because the latter failed to support Negro interests.[16] It should be conceded, however, that Negro loyalty to AFL unions in the South was due mainly to the vested economic interests of Negro AFL union leaders. Furthermore, there was a perceptible difference in the Negroes' reaction in unorganized areas as compared with places where the AFL was already entrenched at the time the CIO was formed. In unorganized areas, the CIO's favorable image amongst Negroes almost always gained for it Negro support, while established benefits and relationships usually caused older organized trades to favor the AFL. Most of the AFL's Negro membership appears to have been in the South, while the CIO made its greatest gains among Negro workers in the Northern automobile, steel, shipbuilding, electrical, and packinghouse industries.

Thus, although some CIO members practiced discrimination, the organization had a very good image in the Negro community when the AFL and the CIO merged in 1956. The Eleventh Constitutional Convention of the CIO in 1950 adopted a resolution "that each CIO affiliate create a Civil Rights Committee, or Department on Fair Practices within its respective organization." The following organizations established such machinery: Amalgamated Clothing Workers; Communications Workers; International Union of Electrical Workers; United Furniture Workers; United Gas, Coke and Chemical Workers; American Newspaper Guild; Oil Workers; United Paperworkers of America; Retail, Wholesale and Department Store Union; United Shoe Workers of America; Transport Workers Union of America; and International Woodworkers of America. Many of these organizations had already established committees by 1950, but they had not assigned specific responsibilities for their day-to-day operation.[17] The transformation in the Negro community's attitudes toward unions during the 1930's was truly remarkable: the New Deal and the CIO succeeded in shifting the attitudes of Negro leaders from antiunion Republicans to prounion Democrats. There was also a great upsurge in Negro union membership during the 1930's. Precise Negro union membership figures are not available, but there were probably at least 1.5 million Negro unionists at the time of the AFL-CIO merger in 1956. Between 1926 and 1928,

when the AFL's total membership was between 2,800,000
and 2,900,000, there were an estimated 61,000 Negroes.[18]
Another estimate put 45,000 Negroes in the AFL in 1930
and another 11,000 in independent unions.[19] In 1940, at
a time when total union membership was 3,392,800, there
were an estimated 500,000 Negro union members.[20] In
1945, the CIO had approximately 400,000 Negroes, or 6.7
percent of its total membership; in the same year the AFL
had about 300,000 Negro members, or about 3.4 percent.
Negroes had constituted about 2.8 percent of the AFL's
1926–28 membership.

Chapter III

THE NEGRO
AND THE AFL-CIO

At the time of the AFL-CIO merger in 1956, race relations in America were undergoing momentous, if not revolutionary, changes. The Negro protest movement was changing from heavy reliance on legal agitation by a relatively few leaders to a mass movement with many militant and competing leaders. After 1900, as we have noted, Southern Negroes were virtually frozen to agriculture and to certain menial nonagricultural jobs; they were trapped by a vicious cycle of discrimination, low incomes, large families, ignorance, and lack of incentives. Even under these conditions, however, Negroes had hope for a better day. True, the vision held out by the Yankees during Reconstruction had proved disappointing, but Booker T. Washington and his followers were convinced that political and social equality could be deferred until hard work, industrial education, and alliances with employers prepared the Negro for competition on an equal basis with whites. While some improvement was possible, most Negroes found only limited escape from their position through industrial education and strikebreaking.

During the time between the Reconstruction period and World War II, the hopes of many Southern Negroes were kept alive by the belief that their conditions could be improved if they crossed over to the promised land beyond Mason and Dixon's line. There they discovered that although segregation was not as rigid as in the South, it was no less real, and the Negro's economic conditions were not always better than they had been in the South. Indeed, in the North many Negroes faced *de facto* job, housing, and school segregation, poverty, inordinately high rates of unemployment, slums, and discrimination untempered by even the slightest traces of *noblesse oblige*.

After Negroes moved to their last bastion of hope in the North and found that wanting, they had a variety of reactions ranging from resignation to desperate militancy and escape from the white man's world through black nationalism. In spite of this mood, however, the militancy of the Negro community undoubtedly also reflected the progress that had been made as well as the obstacles to further advances. Protest is more likely to come from people who have gained the freedom and power to protest than from people who are totally oppressed. This appears in the increasing ability of Negroes to lead militant civil rights movements in the South and by their ability to assume a more aggressive role in Negro-liberal-labor alliances.

AFL-CIO Civil Rights Program

The changing climate of race relations in the United States and the pressures of Negroes and civil rights advocates within the labor movement caused the AFL-CIO to adopt a relatively strong civil rights program. The new federation's constitution listed among its objectives: "To encourage all workers without regard to race, creed, color, national origin or ancestry to share equally in the full benefits of union organization." In order to help the

Executive Council "bring about at the earliest possible date the effective implementation of the principle . . . of nondiscrimination," the AFL-CIO's constitution provided for a Civil Rights Committee (CRC). Day-to-day administration is carried out by a Civil Rights Department.

Although A. Philip Randolph was not at all pleased with the AFL-CIO's failure to impose definite sanctions against discriminating unions,[1] he nevertheless termed the civil rights program of the merged federation a "step forward." [2] When Michael Quill of the CIO Transport Workers Union wanted assurances, before voting for the merger, that the civil rights program would be implemented, CIO President Walter Reuther said, "These are not just words. These will be deeds." [3] Reuther's views were shared by James B. Carey of the International Union of Electrical Workers, who had been chairman of the CIO Civil Rights Committee. Carey said civil rights had been "high on the agenda of the basic principles that concerned the AFL-CIO Unity Committee during its negotiations." [4] Negroes also were reassured by the election of two Negro vice-presidents—A. Philip Randolph, and Willard Townsend of the CIO United Transport Service Employees—and by the fact that Carey, who was highly regarded in the Negro community, was made chairman of the Civil Rights Committee.[5]

However, a number of features of the merger caused Negroes to become increasingly skeptical of the federation's civil rights program. Some Negro leaders noted that unions could be expelled for corruption and communism but not for civil rights violations.[6] This skepticism was strengthened during the first year of the CRC's operations when Carey resigned as chairman because, among other things, he thought the committee was not moving fast enough.[7] Carey was replaced by Charles Zimmerman, vice-president of the International Ladies' Garment Workers Union. Because he was not a union president, Zimmerman's appointment caused further criticism from the NAACP.[8] Zimmerman had long been a leader in the civil rights activities of the Jewish Labor Committee (JLC), which also came under attack from some Negro spokes-men following the merger. The attacks on the JLC were motivated by many factors including its defense of the AFL-CIO; a conviction held by some Negroes that the JLC was mainly interested in the problems of Jews; and a growing feeling that Negroes, and not Jews, should take command of the civil rights movement. Although Zimmerman and the JLC received strong support from such Negro leaders as A. Philip Randolph, Lester Granger of the Urban League, and Roy Wilkins of the NAACP, these attacks caused Zimmerman to resign as chairman of the Civil Rights Committee. He was succeeded by AFL-CIO Secretary-Treasurer William F. Schnitzler in 1961.

Relations between the AFL-CIO and the Negro community were also influenced by the fact that two-thirds of the official positions of the merged organization, including the presidency, went to the AFL, which was never able to overcome its unfavorable image in the Negro community and which never had close relations with organizations such as the NAACP and the NUL. Furthermore, the AFL-CIO Executive Council admitted two unions—the Brotherhood of Locomotive Firemen (BLF) and the Brotherhood of Railway Trainmen (BRT)—to the merged organization even though they still had race bars in their constitutions. Negro-labor relations also were exacerbated by a number of widely publicized cases of legal action against discriminating local unions in Northern cities (Cleveland, Detroit, Philadelphia, San Francisco, Milwaukee, Los Angeles, Hartford, New York, and Washington, D.C.) with large Negro concentrations. At a time of increasing unemployment among Negroes, there was a growing conviction that union discrimination in apprenticeship training and upgrading within plants was at least partly responsible for the Negroes' economic plight.

Role of the National Association
for the Advancement of Colored People

These developments also put a strain on the working relations which had been established between the NAACP and the labor movement. The NAACP's victories in the school desegregation cases increased its prestige in the Negro community, but the changes taking place in race relations made it difficult for it to continue to work closely with organizations like the AFL-CIO that were considered to be discriminatory by increasing numbers of Negroes. Also, the NAACP's position of leadership enabled it to rely more on Negroes and less on unions and liberal whites for financial support. At the same time, however, the NAACP was being challenged in the Negro community by younger and more militant leadership.

These developments made inevitable the fact that the NAACP would become increasingly critical of unions. In December, 1958, NAACP Labor Secretary Herbert Hill, in a memorandum to Boris Shishkin, then the Director of the AFL-CIO Civil Rights Department, filed complaints against locals of the Electrical Workers; Railroad Telegraphers; Plumbers and Pipefitters; Maintenance of Way Employees; Painters, Decorators and Paperhangers; Railway Carmen; Railway Clerks; Boilermakers and Blacksmiths; Pulp, Sulphite and Paper Mill Workers; Sheet Metal Workers; Carpenters and Joiners; and the Paper Makers and Paper Workers. Hill charged that the discriminatory practices of these unions seriously threatened the economic status of Negroes.[9]

The responses of union leaders to these charges, while not uniform, were generally indignant. When questioned, the presidents of most of the unions under specific attack denied the charges or denied responsibility for the conditions outlined in Hill's memorandum. Most of them pointed to changes in their constitutions to prove that their unions did not discriminate.

Negro Union Leaders

The publicity given to the degree of racial discrimination practiced by unions caused Negro trade unionists to become more critical of their organizations. Negroes emphasized that they were demanding, not begging, that white union leaders grant them their rights. As James Jones, a Philadelphia Negro leader, put it:

> We've got to stop Uncle Tomming it. The spotlight is on racial integration and we've got to move while we have the opportunity. If we have to hurt our friends, then we will just have to hurt them. I consider myself to be one of the new breed of Negroes. I'm not begging at the back door for scraps, but knocking on the front door for my rights.[10]

The relations between Negro and white unionists were symbolized by those between George Meany and A. Philip Randolph, the recognized spokesman for Negro unionists. Randolph's long and tireless fight for fair treatment of Negroes by unions and in the larger society and his leadership in the virtually all-Negro Brotherhood of Sleeping Car Porters (BSCP) made him much more independent of whites than other Negro union leaders. The most significant exchange between Meany and Randolph came at the 1959 AFL-CIO convention, in the debates over the expulsion of discriminating unions, the elimination of segregated locals, and the admission of a union accused of discrimination. The BSCP had offered a resolution which would have required that segregated locals "be liquidated and eliminated" by AFL-CIO affiliates. The BSCP delegates argued that segregated locals usually deprived Negroes of equal employment opportunities and that maintaining them was "no more defensible than it was to maintain unions under Communist domination and corrupt influences on the ground the members of said unions desired to keep them." [11] Meany replied heatedly to Randolph: "Is this your idea of a democratic process, that you don't care what the Negro members think? You don't care if they want to maintain the union they have had for so many years? I would like an answer to that." When Randolph answered yes, Meany responded angrily: "That's not my policy. I am for the democratic rights of the Negro members. Who in the hell appointed you as guardian of the Negro members in America? You talk about tolerance!" [12]

The 1959 AFL-CIO convention debates had important consequences for subsequent relations between the federation and the Negro community. Although Randolph, Meany, and a majority of white union leaders apparently paid little attention to Meany's statements, they were reported with indignation in the Negro press.[13]

In 1960, Randolph and other Negro union leaders formed the Negro-American Labor Council (NALC), which sought, among other things, to fight discrimination from within the labor movement. In 1961, Randolph submitted a document to the AFL-CIO Executive Council, which according to one AFL-CIO official "contained a number of charges of discrimination, some general analysis and some programmatic material." [14] A subcommittee of the Executive Council appointed by Meany to study Randolph's charges brought back a report which was regarded by many newspapers as a "censure" of Randolph.[15] In October 1961, the Executive Council adopted the subcommittee report which criticized Randolph for causing "the gap that has developed between organized labor and the Negro community." The report denied Randolph's charges that the AFL-CIO was lax in enforcing its racial policies, accused his BSCP of discriminating against whites, and rejected his proposals that the AFL-CIO adopt a system of penalties against discriminating unions. Voluntary compliance with the principles of equal rights, the council said, would produce a more successful solution to this problem. George Meany said Randolph's attacks on the federation had made the AFL-CIO's civil rights program less effective than it could have been. Randolph had, according to Meany,

> In the last few years . . . become the mouthpiece of the radical few, not the leader as in the past. I resent the fact that he doesn't defend the labor movement. I have admiration for his fight to help his own people, but I also feel he has an obligation to the

trade union movement. He's a union man as well as a Negro.[16]

Randolph answered the Executive Council's report by accusing the AFL-CIO of "moral paralysis, pessimism, defeatism and cynicism." [17] Randolph called the Executive Council subcommittee's report an effort to "brainwash the public into accepting a 'whitewash of labor's do-little civil rights record.' " [18]

Following this conflict, however, relations between Randolph and the AFL-CIO seemed to improve markedly. During the 1961 convention, the "censure" report was referred back to the Executive Council and "buried." [19] Meany also met for two hours with an eighteen-man delegation from the NALC to discuss plans to have the federation take action against discrimination and heal the breach between Meany and Randolph. The 1961 convention strengthened its compliance procedures and adopted a resolution calling for the end of discrimination in all areas, including the labor movement. In what was interpreted as official recognition, Meany accepted an invitation to speak at the NALC's third annual convention in 1962. The AFL-CIO president told the Negro leaders that he had not thought the NALC necessary when it was first formed, "but I respect your motives and share your objectives." [20] Meany explained that he had refused earlier invitations because "frankly, I didn't think I would help solve our problem by going. I probably would have spoken what was on my mind and that might not have been in the interest of a peaceful solution of our troubles." [21]

Randolph told the 1962 NALC delegates that "we are going to maintain our alliance." To emphasize his point, the Negro leader opposed a move by the NALC's New York affiliate to participate in an attack against the International Ladies' Garment Workers Union by Herbert Hill and a subcommittee of the House Committee on Labor and Education. Randolph said, "It is not the function of the NALC to become the ally of any Congressional committee of politicians to help train its guns of investigation through harassment and persecution against the ILGWU, the union of our fellow workers, brothers and sisters." [22] Randolph's defense of the ILGWU was particularly important because union leaders regarded Herbert Hill's attack on that organization, which had acquired a good reputation in regard to its racial practices, as politically inspired. The attacks on the ILGWU, and the NAACP's unsuccessful efforts to decertify an Atlanta local of the Steelworkers, an international which also had a favorable reputation for its racial practices, prompted particularly strong responses from George Meany and Walter Reuther. Some NALC delegates sought unsuccessfully to win the organization's approval of the NAACP's decertification policy, but Randolph told the convention: "I am glad we had the wisdom to reject the doctrine of decertification of unions. . . . When you decertify a union, brother, you are at the mercy of your employer." However, the NALC adopted a resolution supporting the NAACP with the declaration that "this convention views any attacks on the NAACP as ultimately attacks on all of us who support the NAACP." [23]

The NAACP fully supported Hill in his conflicts with the JLC and the ILGWU. The NAACP Board of Directors called on the Special Subcommittee of the House Committee on Education and Labor to "pursue a vigorous and thoroughgoing investigation of racial discrimination" within the ILGWU. The resolution restated Hill's charges against the ILGWU, and concluded that "the union cannot live on its past glories. It must face the reality of its present practices and move to eradicate inequalities."

The dispute between the ILGWU and the NAACP also involved a complaint filed with the New York State Commission for Human Rights (CHR) in 1961, which alleged that a Negro had been denied membership in the ILGWU Local 10 because of his color. However, on May 15, 1963, when the case finally went to a hearing, approximately two hundred Spanish-speaking and Negro members of Local 10 appeared, reportedly prepared to testify on the union's behalf. The ILGWU argued that the complainant had been denied admission to Local 10 not because of his color but because he was not a qualified cutter. After three days of hearings, the charge against the ILGWU local was withdrawn on the basis of a joint stipulation under which the union agreed:

> In line with its oft asserted and regular policy . . . against discrimination . . . that it will, on the same basis as it applies to all other applicants for admission to membership, exercise its good offices in assisting the complainant to become a qualified cutter and to gain admission to membership in this union.[24]

The NAACP's conflict with the ILGWU apparently had been terminated by 1965, when the association's executive secretary, Roy Wilkins, addressed the ILGWU's convention. Wilkins, who was in Europe at the time the NAACP board called for the investigation of the ILGWU, said that he had had detailed discussions with leaders of the Garment Workers and he praised the union's "long-standing commitment to political and industrial democracy" which made the NAACP leader confident of an "honest and forthright assault on the remaining pockets of proscription within the labor movement and, if any be found, within its own union." [25]

The Rapprochement

Thus, in spite of some bitterness during the years following the merger, relations between the AFL-CIO and various Negro, civil rights, and labor leaders were much improved by 1966. The conflicts had been due, in part, to the restructuring of relations because of the merger and changes in the Negro community. These changing relations focused attention on the problem of discrimination by unions. Improvement in Negro-union relations came about partly because of better understanding and partly because of the mutual dependence of Negroes and unions. Understanding came because as a result of their conflict with unions Negroes learned more about the structure of the labor movement, and particularly the fact that the AFL-CIO actually has limited power to change the practices of its national and local affiliates. Moreover, the passage of civil rights legislation caused the AFL-CIO to have more power to abolish discrimination in its ranks.

The AFL-CIO's decisive support of civil rights legislation also strengthened its position in the Negro community. The publicity given to racial discrimination, and the undeniable fact that widespread discrimination existed in craft unions on the railroads and in the building, printing, and skilled machinists trades, changed the AFL-CIO's posture from one of defensiveness to one of advocating measures to eliminate discrimination. The debates over union racial practices also gave AFL-CIO leaders a better understanding of the Negro community's changed attitudes toward some forms of discrimination—such as segregated locals—which formerly had been more acceptable to Negroes. Union leaders also gained a better understanding of the pressures and problems confronting civil rights leaders. Negro leaders have, moreover, noted the similarity between the tradition of the civil rights movement and the tradition of the labor movement and the common objectives (and enemies) which continue to bind them together despite their differences. For example, Rev. Martin Luther King told the 1962 UAW convention:

> There are more ties of kinship between labor and the Negro people than tradition . . . labor needs a wage-hour bill . . . Negroes need the same measures, even more desperately . . . Labor needs housing legislation . . . Negroes need housing legislation also. Labor needs an adequate old-age medical bill and so do Negroes . . . What labor needs, Negroes need; and simple logic therefore puts us side by side in the struggle for all elements in a decent standard of living.[26]

Similarly, Clarence Mitchell, director of the NAACP's Washington Bureau, told the Maryland and District of Columbia AFL-CIO convention in August 1965 that in the passage of civil rights legislation in the Eighty-eighth and Eighty-ninth congresses, "organized labor gave unfailing,

consistent and massive support where it counted most. . . .
It is frequently necessary to work nights, Sundays and
holidays to achieve our objectives. The members of organized labor were always present at the right time and
in the right places." In turn, the NAACP and other civil
rights organizations have fought for such union objectives
as the repeal of Section 14(b) of the Taft-Hartley Act
which makes the so-called state "right-to-work" laws
possible.[27]

It thus becomes clear that the breach that developed
between the AFL-CIO and some Negro leaders in the years
following the merger of the unions had been partially
closed by the 1960's. One important factor that improved
Negro-union relations was the realization by many civil
rights leaders and labor leaders that their mutual objectives
and common enemies were more important than the factors
that divided them.

Few civil rights leaders doubted the value of the AFL-
CIO's help in achieving the Negro's political objectives or
questioned the union's sincerity in its attempt to implement its civil rights policies. It became increasingly clear,
moreover, that the AFL-CIO's power over its affiliates was
rather limited and that the main problem of discrimination
was at the local and national union levels. The federation's
relations with the National Urban League and the Negro
American Labor Council seemed especially improved by
1966, when the NUL entered into an agreement with the
AFL-CIO to undertake a program to enhance the job and
promotion opportunities of Negroes and the NALC announced that it was shifting from its earlier position of
attacking the AFL-CIO to one of alliance and cooperation.
The AFL-CIO's relations with the NAACP also were improved, although there was considerable mistrust and
mutual antipathy between the association's labor secretary
and the federation's leaders.

The foregoing does not mean, however, that there will
not be continuing differences between the AFL-CIO and
Negro leaders. A continuing source of tension between
unions and Negroes will undoubtedly be the different

priorities they attach to the same objectives. Union leaders and civil rights leaders also will have differences because of personality clashes and misunderstandings. Of course, a major conflict between the AFL-CIO and civil rights leaders is likely to continue to be the difficulties involved in eliminating discrimination in some of the federation's affiliates.

Chapter IV

UNION RACIAL PROBLEMS
IN THE SOUTH

Since trade unions tend to reflect their environment, it is not surprising that the race problem was a preoccupation of early unions in the South. The general pattern seems to have been for local unions to exclude Negroes wher-ever they could. And, where Negroes were too numerous or too strategically located to be excluded, they were accepted into segregated locals or, rarely, allowed to join on an integrated basis with whites. Although racially integrated unions violated prevailing racial sentiment in the South, some unions, like the New Orleans Brick-layers, have a history of integration dating back to the 1860's. The Coal Miners seem to have had the most per-sistent policy of integration in the South, perhaps because their geographical isolation gave them a certain immunity from social pressures. Nevertheless, as late as the 1930's, the Mine Workers' racial policies caused them to be criticized by segregationist community and union leaders in Alabama. As noted earlier, the CIO followed the UMW's policy of organizing integrated locals in the South. Those unions which did not bar Negroes entirely usually organized them in segregated or auxiliary locals. This policy was followed by the Knights of Labor, the Carpenters, Painters, Longshoremen, Tobacco Workers, Musicians, and the unions in the pulp and paper industry. Although CIO unions rarely chartered separate locals for Negroes, segregation in seating and social affairs was common.

The unions in the South which usually excluded Negroes were those railroad organizations with formal racial bars, the craft unions in the printing trades, and such building trades unions as the Asbestos Workers, the Elevator Constructors, the Plumbers, the Pipefitters, and the Sheet Metal Workers. A few CIO unions excluded Negroes from membership, but this was very rare and almost always was opposed by the CIO and its international affiliates.

Industrialization was a particularly important factor in the undermining of segregation and discrimination in the South, because it brought Negroes and whites into close contact on the job, intensified competition between Negroes and whites for jobs, made Negroes aware of their need for better education and equal political rights, and exposed the South's racial practices to worldwide scrutiny. The growing size and influence of Negro communities outside the South greatly increased Negro political power, especially at the Federal level. As will be seen, however, the factors tending to erode job segregation worked against great obstacles and at a very slow pace; this was true even after World War II.

Since the AFL-CIO merger coincided with a period of growing racial ferment in the South caused by the 1954 Supreme Court school desegregation decision, the federation faced a serious dilemma. It wanted to expand unionization into the relatively unorganized South, but was afraid that its equalitarian racial position, which it was compelled to follow in the North, would alienate Southern union members and impede organizing activities in that region. Although the federation proceeded with some caution during the period of active and widespread opposition to integration in the South, it did not modify its equalitarian position in order to cater to the South. Moreover, almost every Southern state federation of labor supported the AFL-CIO's official position and several of them vigorously opposed the segregationists, even when this opposition caused local unions to disaffiliate.[1]

Segregationist Labor Organizations

One of the anti-integrationist labor organizations formed in the wake of the Supreme Court's 1954 school desegregation decision was the United Southern Employees Association (USEA), chartered in North Carolina in 1956. Subsequently chartered as a corporation also in Virginia, Alabama, Florida, Georgia, South Carolina, and North Carolina, the USEA made a strong appeal to employers by encouraging "cooperation and fair dealing," as well as anti-integrationist policies.[2]

According to a USEA leader, "The great majority of USEA members are ex-AFL-CIO union members who have quit the AFL-CIO because of [its] race-baiting tactics. . . . We believe that southerners should organize and control their own unions just as we elect our own congressmen from the South to represent us in Congress. We don't need northern rabble rousers to represent us in labor." [3]

In one episode, the USEA sought to organize many workers who were members of both the Ku Klux Klan and the Textile Workers Union, but the workers' loyalty to the union apparently was stronger than USEA leaders thought. The USEA wanted to form an alliance with the Klan, but when the USEA founder criticized the CIO at a KKK meeting, union members protested that they had come to talk about the "colored and white" and not to discuss "our union." [4] Because it advocated cooperation with employers and had attempted to break a strike at Rock Hill, South Carolina, the USEA was considered to be a "scab outfit" by the unionized textile workers.

The USEA apparently generated more publicity and controversy than membership, and although it was active in a number of places, it apparently did not succeed in winning bargaining rights or in establishing permanent labor organizations. Its chief support appears to have been limited mainly to the Piedmont, but it is reported to have moved into Birmingham after another segregationist group —the Southern Aircraft Workers (SAW)—failed to win bargaining rights from the UAW at Hayes Aircraft between 1956 and 1958. Some of the UAW's staunchest segregationist members vigorously opposed the SAW.

Segregationists also tried to form a Southern Federation of Labor in July 1956, "to drive the AFL-CIO back North with its notions of integration." However, its meager support caused the SFL to die aborning. After only about 135 and 250 persons, respectively (including many "observers"), attended two "mass" meetings in Birmingham, it was announced that the SFL would concentrate on boring from within existing unions rather than forming separate organizations. Little has subsequently been heard from this organization.

The Southern Crafts, Inc., headed by a railroad engineer from Birmingham, was another attempt at a dual labor movement. One of the main reasons the members of this organization claimed to have withdrawn from the AFL-CIO was that they didn't "feel that they can remain a part of an organization that will take its members' money and force integration upon the South." [5] The Southern Crafts, like the USEA, supported laws restricting union security because "The Surest Way to maintain segregation in Alabama and the South for those who earn a living by the sweat of their brow is to preserve our right to work laws." [6] The writer's attempts to establish contact with the leaders of Southern Crafts in order to secure membership figures were unsuccessful. It would appear, however, that the organization had very few members even in the Birmingham area.

The policy of the Southern States Conference of Union People (SSCUP), formed by a group of Chattanooga unionists, was to work from within the regular unions in an effort to educate the AFL-CIO to anti-integrationist policies. The founding committee adopted a resolution which declared the AFL-CIO to be,

> Under the control of labor leaders who are aiding and abetting the mixing of the White and Negro races in our public schools and elsewhere, and . . . have contributed many thousands of dollars to the NAACP, an organization dedicated to the elimination of our Southern principle of segregation, and . . . Walter Reuther is a member of the Board of Directors of the NAACP, an organization that is Communist influenced and dedicated to destroying our Southern civilization. . . .[7]

The SSCUP also apparently died soon after it was organized.

Although they were not avowedly antiunion, both the White Citizens' Council and the Ku Klux Klan sought to infiltrate Southern unions. The main leader of the Mississippi White Citizens' Council movement said that the WCC was not antilabor but prosegregation and if Mississippi labor was prosegregation, "then we are together."[8] While the WCC was not avowedly antilabor, there is no question of its opposition to national union leaders and the AFL-CIO's racial policies. The WCC's main policy with respect to unions was infiltration and opposition from within.

The Ku Klux Klan became particularly active following the failure of so-called legal measures to prevent desegregation. The Klan had long been a factor in Southern unions, but relatively little was heard from it when the WCC was at its peak and when it looked like the Councils' "legalistic" approach might succeed. But the defeat of "legalism" destroyed it as an alternative, causing some of the radicals to turn to the Klan. And, since most of the Klan's membership has been made up of workers, farmers, and small businessmen, it is not surprising that the KKK has been a source of some concern to labor leaders. Until the early 1960's the Klan apparently was most active in the Birmingham and Tuscaloosa areas of Alabama and in Florida, Georgia, North and South Carolina, and in eastern Tennessee, especially around the Chattanooga and Knoxville areas. The Klan later mushroomed in Mississippi and north Louisiana, where the WCC had had its greatest strength.

Although union leaders discount the KKK's claim that trade union members constitute half of the Klan's membership, they admit that by 1966 the KKK had become a serious threat in some places. Moreover, union members have held important positions in the hooded order, especially in Alabama and Georgia. One of the main leaders of the KKK is a former member of the Rubber Workers at Tuscaloosa, Alabama. The Klan has long had considerable strength among Tuscaloosa rubber workers and gets active support from members of the Steelworkers' locals around Birmingham. Most of the KKK leaders in the Bessemer and Birmingham areas are union members. The KKK is also reported to have drawn much of its support from Birmingham building trades and railroad unions. The Mississippi Grand Dragon in 1965 was a member of the Teamsters. In Georgia, where the Klan has long been influential within the labor movement, several KKK leaders have been drawn from the Auto Workers' locals in Atlanta; for instance, the Georgia Grand Dragon in 1965 was a UAW member. Perhaps because many paper mills are located in rural areas in order to be close to supplies of pulp wood, paper mill towns often have been centers of Klan strength. The Klan has, therefore, been active in the Pulp, Sulphite, and Papermakers unions. International representatives of the Papermakers reported in 1965 that the Klan had become particularly active in Mississippi and Louisiana locals.

Although it is impossible to determine the exact number of Klansmen who are union members, the proportion probably is very small. Even if the KKK's claim of 25,000 union members is granted, total Klan membership within the South's unions would be only about 1 percent of the total membership. It is highly unlikely, however, that the

Klan's active union membership is as high as 25,000. Nevertheless, union leaders concede that the KKK is a real threat to some local unions. Because of their tactics of intimidation, threats, and violence, even a very small number of Klansmen have a great capacity for mischief. Moreover, until recently the Klan was able to practice these tactics with a certain impunity because members of this so-called "invisible empire" were rarely brought to justice for their deeds.

Another source of trouble for unions in the South has been opposition to racial equality by union members. The state federations have many Negro union members, have political objectives requiring general community support, and have generally been very outspoken in their support for civil rights causes. At the same time, however, the federations are vulnerable to withdrawals because local unions do not need to be affiliated with the state federations and with city central bodies in order to carry on their main collective bargaining activities. For example, the Chattanooga Central Labor Union was bitterly criticized by segregationist union leaders for endorsing the local school board's plans to comply with the Supreme Court's desegregation decision. The CLU's action, which was prompted by a 1954 AFL convention resolution endorsing the Supreme Court's decision, evoked vicious attacks from segregationist unions led by the Printing Pressmen and joined by the Switchmen, Carpenters, Plumbers, Machinists, Typographical, and Brotherhood of Electrical Workers locals. The CLU and the *Labor World,* the local labor paper, were accused of being under the domineering control of leaders "supporting organizations and sociological theories . . . dedicated to removing the last vestiges of our Southern heritage" and "selling us out for 30 pieces of our own silver" by contributing union money to the NAACP. Local union leaders also were denounced as "alien Communist lovers and socializers who have had their way for a long time." According to the segregationists, the CLU could not deny "some responsibility for the disgusting integration of Negro and white workers in the labor movement in Tennessee." [9] As a result of this criticism, some locals withdrew from the CLU, and some members dropped their subscriptions to *Labor World*, and the central body's support of the school board was rescinded.

A number of international unions also have had trouble implementing their racial policies in the South. The Auto Workers revoked the charter of a Dallas local in 1952 for refusing to follow the international's racial policies, and it has had considerable difficulty with locals in Memphis and Atlanta. The Memphis International Harvester local was placed under trusteeship by the UAW in 1960 after a long series of disputes between the local and the international over racial matters, in particular, the local's segregation of facilities in its headquarters and strikes by local whites to prevent International Harvester from upgrading Negroes and using them in nontraditional jobs. However, the company and the international union took firm positions and forced the local whites to comply with company and union policies. Union and company policies succeeded, in this case, because of relatively high wages in the plant and the fact that the international was certified as bargaining agent by the NLRB.

The only Negroes in the automobile plant organized by the UAW at Atlanta in 1937 were janitors but the local whites refused to accept these Negro workers into the local until forced to do so by the international union in 1946. Even after the Negroes were accepted into the union, seating at union meetings was segregated. During the racial ferment of the 1950's and 1960's the company hired more Negroes and moved them into jobs previously held by whites.

No union has followed more vigorously equalitarian racial policies in the South than the United Packinghouse Workers (UPWA). The UPWA's policy was dictated by the necessity of organizing the large number of Negroes in the industry, many of whom had broken in initially as strikebreakers. The UPWA's policies have been opposed in the South and it has lost a few locals for this reason. On balance, however, the UPWA's support from Negroes has caused it to gain more members than it has lost by defections from whites. In 1954, for example, Louisiana UPWA leaders endeavored to get nine sugar locals to withdraw from the Packinghouse Workers, partly because of the union's racial policies. But the international was able to avert the secession of five of its largest locals with Negro majorities by reminding them of the union's equalitarian position. Four smaller locals withdrew, but two of these returned to the UPWA because they could not survive alone and could find no strong union willing to take them. The UPWA also encountered opposition from Southern whites in Georgia, Alabama, and Texas because of its racial policies.

Some unions have lost Southern locals because of racial policies; the American Federation of Teachers lost five locals and the National Association of Letter Carriers lost one when these locals refused to obey international mandates to desegregate local unions. All Southern state AFL-CIO federations apparently have lost some affiliates for racial reasons. The hardest hit seem to have been Mississippi and Alabama. Alabama union leaders reported in 1965 that they had lost the affiliation of 36,000 members for racial reasons, and of 50,000 union members in Mississippi only 19,000 were affiliated with the state AFL-CIO in 1965.

Union leaders have been afraid that their support of civil rights causes would impede organizational efforts in the South. The open segregationist sentiments of Southern workers and the widespread use of racial arguments against unions in elections for representation would seem to make these fears plausible. Antiunion campaigns, especially in rural areas, have stressed trade union support of integration and financial contributions to the NAACP or other civil rights organizations.

In spite of these factors, however, an examination of a number of organizing campaigns in which the race issue was used against unions, and discussions with union organizers in the South over a number of years, leads to the conclusion that these arguments have not been very significant in causing unions to lose elections they might otherwise have won. Perhaps racial arguments have been important in a few cases where union and antiunion forces were about evenly divided. But this issue has been exaggerated by newspaper publicity; also, workers who are afraid to join unions—or who see no need to do so— frequently use the unions' integrationist positions as excuses for not joining. Similarly, union organizers who have failed to organize a plant find the race issue a convenient excuse for their failure.

The evidence supports the conclusion that if workers are convinced that unions are beneficial in their particular situations they will give little weight to the organization's racial policies in making their decisions to join a union. Some union organizers have even reported that civil rights demonstrations in the South have actually helped their organizing efforts. Frank Parker, assistant Southern director for the Retail, Wholesale and Department Store Workers, reported that civil rights demonstrators caused whites to be more inclined to organize. According to Parker:

> Workers have seen these demonstrations and picket-lines involving civil rights and some responded by saying, "If they can get away with it, why can't we?" Of course, this is not new with many Negro workers. They have joined and fought for our union in the past. But the demonstrations have helped to spur them on, to encourage them to look for the union to help them. I would say that in South Georgia in the Macon area, and in South Alabama where we've been organizing, we probably would not have been successful if it hadn't been for the demonstrations in Albany, Georgia . . . some employers use the civil rights agitation against our union, sometimes successfully . . . Of course, most often this type of attack doesn't help the boss at all.[10]

Organizers have noted, however, that although the race issue might not have been a very important factor in keeping whites from voting for unions, there is a tendency in some sections of the South for Negroes to give less support to unions than they have in the past. Until 1957–58 unions almost always felt that they would have Negro support in organizing campaigns. Since then, however, some elections have been lost for lack of Negro backing. In the main, however, unions with good reputations among Negroes have been actively supported by Rev. Martin Luther King and other civil rights leaders. In 1964, for example, King and other Southern Christian Leadership Conference leaders actively supported a chemical workers' strike against the Scripto Company in Atlanta and thereby aided materially in its successful resolution.

Political Action

Informal Negro-labor coalitions are being formed in several Southern states, sometimes with the aid of liberals or other minority groups. In Texas, a formal coalition was established among Negro, labor, Mexican-American, and liberal groups in 1963. Since Negroes and Mexican-Americans made up about 30 percent of the Texas population in 1960, labor leaders hope that the liberal coalition can eventually gain control of the Texas Democratic party. This hope is based upon the assumption that the growth of the Republican party will split whites along economic lines, giving a liberal-labor-Negro-Latin coalition the balance of political power. Growing urbanization, increasing union membership, and legislative reapportionment are all expected to increase the power of this coalition. Of course, there is also the assumption that the forces which unite the groups in the coalition are more important than the differences that pull them apart.

If the increasing number of Negro voters strengthens Negro-labor political coalitions, segregationists are afraid the balance of political power will swing away from them. They consider it important, therefore, to fight unions or to gain union support for segregationist measures. One effective technique for splitting Negro-labor coalitions in some places has been to support prolabor segregationists for public office.

To conclude, racial unrest probably has had little effect on union organizing. Surprisingly few locals or members have withdrawn from AFL-CIO unions for racial reasons, and the segregationist labor organizations have achieved relatively little success in the South. The main effects of racist activity appear to have been to cause some disaffiliations from state and local labor federations. The main long-run effect of racial differences in the South probably will be in Negro-union political alliances. These conclusions rest upon the following considerations:

Segregationist labor organizations have been relatively unsuccessful because of inadequate leadership. There seems to have been no case in which a regular union leader has been willing to leave his position to lead one of the racist groups. Southern unionists seem to see no inconsistency in simultaneously supporting the UAW and the KKK; they give allegiance to both the WCC type of organization and to trade unions because they believe national union leaders are interested mainly in the politico-economic aspects of unionism and will not push integration in the South, a conclusion based on the experiences of most unions in that region.

Economic influences encourage union members to continue their allegiance to national unions. The most important unions in the South are craft organizations, railroad brotherhoods, and industrial unions which are associated with strongly organized bases outside the South. Where they attribute their good conditions to unions, Southerners apparently will not lightly sacrifice their jobs or unions to their prejudices. Except in rare cases, unions which lost Southern locals primarily for racial reasons were not effective collective bargaining organizations.

Finally, race trouble in the unions seems most likely to occur where there is race trouble in the community, when groups like the KKK or Citizens' Councils raise the issue in local union affairs, and when integrationist activities of national union leaders are widely publicized. Whites often break with Southern tradition when they join unions and will rarely risk complete ostracism by becoming identified as integrationists. They therefore feel compelled to publicly repudiate equalitarian racial statements and actions by national leaders, especially when challenged by anti-integrationist organizations. It would be a mistake, however, to assume that these public declarations portend withdrawal from the union.

It would also be a mistake to assume that the racist activities of the Klan and other organizations are representative of the workers of the South. Even at the peak of reaction to the Supreme Court's desegregation decisions, only a very small fraction of union members openly opposed the integrationist policies of the AFL-CIO or their national unions. Moreover, the passage of the Civil Rights Act of 1964 and other civil rights legislation has caused union opposition to equal job opportunities to diminish. The attitude of Southern union members seems to be that "whether we like it or not integration is the law of the land so let's adjust to it." The activities of the KKK are probably the last act of a dying institution. And, although there will be some resistance to integration by some craft unionists in the South, this resistance probably will be no greater than it has been in Pittsburgh, Cleveland, Milwaukee, Philadelphia, San Francisco, or Detroit.

Chapter V

RACIAL PRACTICES
OF NATIONAL
AND LOCAL UNIONS

It has already been demonstrated that union racial practices, responsive to prevailing social and economic conditions, tend to reflect the quality of race relations in communities where their members live, and what is considered "acceptable" practice at one time may be considered unacceptable later. Around 1900, for example, unions would have incurred strong opposition from Southern communities if they had accepted Negroes and whites on an equal basis in the same unions, but by World War II—and partly because of the CIO's policies—integrated locals existed throughout the South. Yet, the fact that some unions in the South accepted Negroes on an integrated basis as early as the 1860's while some Northern unions continued to follow racist practices suggests that factors other than prevailing racial attitudes influence union racial practices.

It has also been observed in connection with the causes of union racial practices that the federations were less likely to discriminate than their local affiliates. This suggests that union structure is one factor in union racial discrimination. The federations have objectives which require Negro support, whereas some national and local unions feel that the admission of Negroes into their organizations would conflict with the attainment of certain objectives.

The diversity of union racial practices suggests that the causes of union discrimination are not randomly distributed throughout the labor movement. If they were, one would find such practices as racial exclusion randomly distributed among the national unions, but the fact that exclusion is concentrated in certain kinds of unions suggests that specific rather than random causes are at work. Some of these specific factors influencing national and local unions may be considered by examining two important forms of discrimination, namely, (1) *exclusion* of Negroes from union membership by formal and informal means, and (2) *segregation*.

Formal Exclusion

Negroes may be excluded from membership in unions by formal or informal means. The first takes the form of constitutional law or other explicit means of restricting membership to whites. Informal exclusion takes the form of tacit agreements among union members and officers that Negroes will not be accepted.

Although the exact number is not known with certainty, in 1930 there were at least 26 national unions which barred Negroes from membership by formal means.[1] By 1943, mergers and changing racial practices had reduced the number of restrictive unions to about 14, 7 of which were AFL affiliates: Machinists; Switchmen's Union of North America; Railway Telegraphers; Masters, Mates and Pilots; Railway Mail Association; Wire Weavers Protective Association; and the Airline Pilots Association. The following organizations with formal racial restrictions were not affiliated with the AFL: Locomotive Engineers; Locomotive Firemen, Railway Trainmen; Railway Yardmasters of America; Railway Yardmasters of North America; Order of Railway Conductors; and the Train Dispatchers Association. By 1949 the number of unions with formal race bars had been reduced to 9, 1 of which, the Railway Telegraphers, was a member of the AFL. The Railway Telegraphers removed their race bar in 1952. The AFL-CIO would have had no affiliate with a race bar if it had not admitted the formerly independent Railway Trainmen and Locomotive Firemen to the federation. These organizations removed their race bars in 1960 and 1963, respectively.

It will be noted that almost all the unions with formal race bars were associated with the transportation industry. The sources of discrimination in the railroads are not wholly clear, but probably include the following:

1. Many railroad organizations were formed in the South or border states (Machinists, Maintenance of Way Employees, Boilermakers, Railway Telegraphers, and Railway Clerks). Their constitutions frequently restricted membership to white men of "good moral character, temperate habits" [2] or "white born, of good moral character, sober and industrious." [3] When these organizations were formed, they undoubtedly considered that their "status" would have been jeopardized by admitting Negroes. These constitutional provisions are obviously based on the idea of white "superiority and competence." [4]

2. Early railroad unions were fraternal and social organizations, formed at a time when it was not considered proper to have social relations with Negroes.

3. Many of these unions started as insurance societies at a time when many insurance companies considered the transportation business too risky and also regarded Negroes as poorer risks than whites.

4. Jobs on the railroads were "prestige" jobs, which by definition could not go to Negroes. Negroes held many firemen's jobs until technological changes made these jobs easier and cleaner; they then became "white" jobs;

however, the Brotherhood of Locomotive Firemen was prevented by the Federal courts from excluding Negroes from firemen's jobs.

Unions began to abandon exclusion by formal means, or to adopt more subtle forms, due to the following: expansion of Negro employment in jurisdictions covered by these unions, especially during World Wars I and II; competition between unions for Negro votes in representation election; embarrassment of exclusionist union leaders at conventions and in the press by criticism from Negro and white union leaders, especially the moral castigations from within the AFL by the Negro leaders of the Brotherhood of Sleeping Car Porters; action by such governmental agencies as the wartime and state FEP committees; and fear of the loss of exclusive bargaining rights, union shop provisions, or other legal privileges under the Railway Labor Act or the Taft-Hartley Act. The experiences of the Railway Clerks, Boilermakers, and Machinists unions illustrate the play of these factors.

BROTHERHOOD OF RAILWAY AND STEAMSHIP CLERKS

The founders of the Brotherhood of Railway Clerks (BRSC), following the pattern of other railroad unions, included a "white only" clause in the union's 1899 constitution.[5] The BRSC's racial barrier led to difficulties during World War I, when the union expanded its jurisdiction to take in freight-handlers, many of whom were Negroes. The Negro freight-handlers were organized into federal locals attached directly to the AFL, but this arrangement proved unsatisfactory to both the BRSC and the Negro workers. The Clerks lost dues and the freight-handlers were relegated to an inferior status and were inadequately represented. The Negroes asked either for a national charter or to be admitted on an equal basis with the Clerks; the BRSC refused to permit either of these alternatives. As a consequence, many Negroes refused to join the federal locals.

With the upsurge in union organization during the 1930's, the Railway Clerks again became interested in organizing the Negro freight-handlers. But since both the Negroes and the international union continued to be dissatisfied with the practice of chartering federal locals, the BRSC Executive Council was authorized by its 1939 convention to put the Negro workers into auxiliary locals represented by white officers. Despite the Negroes' bitter protests to both the AFL Executive Council and the 1940 AFL convention, they again were denied a national charter and were transferred to the BRSC. This action was taken after BRSC President George Harrison assured the AFL Executive Council that the previous convention of his union had taken action "for the affiliation of these workers with full rights and privileges." [6] After the Negroes protested the auxiliary status to which they were being assigned without their consent, President William Green told the 1940 AFL convention that "these men will be members of the Brotherhood of Railway Clerks and fully entitled to enjoy the rights and privileges of the Brotherhood of Railway Clerks." [7] These promises were not kept, however, and the Negroes were relegated to the position of auxiliaries, remaining so until after the New York law against discrimination was passed in 1945.

In 1946, after the New York State Commission Against Discrimination (SCAD) informed the Clerks and other railroad unions that auxiliaries and constitutional color bars violated the New York law, George Harrison appointed a committee which included prominent Southern members who recommended to the 1947 BRSC convention that the race bar be removed. Although some delegates vigorously opposed this move, Harrison gave assurances that these formal changes were really not going to alter things very much, and the delegates voted to strike the word "white" from the BRSC constitution. Negroes were then advised that they could join the white lodges, and by June 1950, a SCAD investigator found only four auxiliary BRSC lodges left in New York and New Jersey.

The legal status of the BRSC's auxiliary lodges was also weakened by the 1951 amendment to the Railway Labor Act permitting the union shop. After the passage of this

amendment, the BRSC was eager to have Negroes join, but
could not use union shop provisions to require them to do
so if they did not have equal conditions of membership.
After the auxiliary locals were abolished, many BRSC
locals (150) continued to be virtually all-Negro, but by
1964 these were being eliminated because of many pressures, including state fair employment laws and the Federal
government contract committees. The union argued that
the existence of all-Negro lodges was due to employer
hiring practices and that they happened to be all-Negro
because locals are organized along jurisdictional lines.
However, the foregoing description of the development of
the BRSC's racial policies casts doubt on this argument.

BOILERMAKERS

In 1908, after debating about whether to leave the
racial bar in their constitution or transfer it to the ritual,
the Boilermakers decided in favor of the constitutional
bar. In 1937, however, some Southerners sought to remove
the bar, not because they wanted to "defend the Negro"
but because the lower wages paid unorganized Negroes
threatened union conditions. In response, in 1937 the
Boilermakers gave the Executive Committee authority to
establish auxiliary lodges for Negroes. The Executive Committee used the auxiliary device during the early days of
World War II, when Negroes flocked to the coasts to take
jobs in the shipyards. Naturally, the Negroes protested this
treatment, and they refused to join the inferior unions.
The Boilermakers forced a showdown when they attempted
to enforce their closed shop agreements and have Negroes
discharged for refusing to join the auxiliaries. The Negro
workers then turned for help to various governmental
agencies, including the NLRB, the Fair Employment Practices Committee (FEPC), and the courts.

A series of actions followed. The FEPC held hearings,
found the auxiliaries discriminatory, and ordered the union
and the companies to cease and desist.[8] But the international officers refused to obey the FEPC's order,[9] even
though President Roosevelt urged the international's offi-

cers and AFL President Green to end discrimination in the union.[10] The Negro workers also failed to get relief from the NLRB, which refused to issue a direct ruling against the auxiliary. Relief finally came from the California Supreme Court which decided, in a number of cases, that the union could not enforce the closed shop against members of the auxiliary locals.[11] Following these decisions, several shipyards announced that they would no longer discharge Negroes for refusing to join the auxiliaries. Faced with this possible loss of revenue and economic control, the Boilermakers' Executive Committee authorized the elimination of auxiliary locals.

INTERNATIONAL ASSOCIATION OF MACHINISTS

The International Association of Machinists (IAM) formally barred Negroes from 1888, when the International was organized in Atlanta, until 1948, when the bar was removed. The forces changing the IAM's practices were similar to those which were eroding the race bars in the BRSC and the Boilermakers: the race bar was transferred from the constitution to the ritual as a condition of admission to the AFL in 1895; the IAM lost some of its Southern character as it spread from Georgia to areas outside the South; the racial bar limited the Machinists' expansion and increasingly embarrassed its officers; the growth of Negro employment in the railroad shops during and after World War I caused the IAM to urge the AFL to organize Negroes into federal locals; competition increased between the IAM and the United Automobile Workers-CIO for Negro membership in the aircraft industry during and after World War II; charges were filed against the IAM with the wartime FEPC;[12] the International's leaders were embarrassed by a discussion of their racial practices in the U.S. Senate;[13] IAM officers also were concerned because the race bar was being cited by unions —especially the Teamsters—as grounds for the NLRB to deny the Machinists the right to represent Negroes;[14] and finally, the IAM was afraid it might lose bargaining rights because of the state FEPC laws and the Taft-Hartley law.

As was true of the Railway Clerks and the Boiler-makers, the IAM continued to have segregated locals after 1948.

Informal Exclusion

The decline in formal exclusion by international unions does not mean that discrimination has declined, because local affiliates of these unions, as well as others which never had formal race bars, exclude Negroes by a number of informal means. These include agreements not to sponsor Negroes for membership; refusal to admit Negroes into apprenticeship programs or to accept their applications, or simply to ignore their applications; general "understandings" to vote against Negroes if they are proposed (for example, as few as three members of some locals can bar applicants for membership); refusal of journey-man status to Negroes by means of examinations which either are not given to whites or are rigged so that Negroes cannot pass them; exertion of political pressure on governmental licensing agencies to ensure that Negroes fail the tests; and restriction of membership to sons, nephews, or other relatives of members.

BUILDING TRADES

Although exclusion from union membership is a serious problem in the construction industry where unions control jobs, it should be emphasized that the racial practices of the different building trades vary considerably and that as a whole the building trades are certainly no more reprehensible than the many employers who refuse to hire Negroes for white collar and supervisory positions. Moreover, the building trades' record has been no worse than that of the railroad unions, which have used their bargaining power to exclude Negroes entirely from jobs as engineers and conductors and to require the removal of Negro locomotive firemen. There is likewise little evidence that the printing trades have been any more open to Negroes than the construction crafts.

What makes the construction unions more important than some others is the fact that, for a number of reasons, attention has been focused on discrimination in that industry. For one thing, construction employment is expected to expand while employment on the railroads is expected to remain stable or to decline. In addition, many Negroes are employed in the building trades, which causes attention to be focused on those related crafts which have very few or no Negroes. Negroes have been particularly concerned about the virtual absence of their youngsters from many of the apprenticeship training programs which provide entry into the skilled crafts. (See Table 5.1.)

The construction crafts that have had the fewest Negro members have been the electricians, plumbers, glaziers, pipefitters, iron workers, steamfitters, sheet metal workers, and elevator constructors. Indeed, there are virtually no Negroes in the unionized sectors of these crafts in any Southern city and outside of a few exceptions, the most notable of which is New York, there are very few in most Northern or Western cities. The International Union of Operating Engineers has a reputation for barring Negroes in such places as Denver, San Francisco, and Los Angeles, but has been regarded as one of the best construction unions in Washington, D.C. Similarly, the Teamsters have integrated their locals in such Southern cities as Atlanta and New Orleans, while they are generally regarded as discriminatory on the West Coast, especially in the brewery and dairy industries but, again, are regarded as one of the least discriminatory unions in St. Louis.[15] The Bricklayers have also acquired a good racial reputation in most places, but in 1957 Local 8 of that organization in Milwaukee accepted two Negro members only after extensive publicity, legal action, and a threat of expulsion from the international union. In most places in the South, even where the Bricklayers have segregated locals, that organization is regarded as one of the best building trades unions with respect to its treatment of Negro members; indeed, the Bricklayers have for many years had a constitutional provision that requires a $100 fine

TABLE 5.1

Negro Apprentices by Occupation, 1950 and 1960

	NEGRO APPRENTICES IN THE EXPERIENCED CIVILIAN LABOR FORCE					
	TOTAL		NUMBER		PERCENTAGE OF TOTAL	
OCCUPATION	1950	1960	1950	1960	1950	1960
Total apprentices	115,440	86,966	2,190	2,191	1.90%	2.52%
Auto mechanics	3,660	1,761	120	40	3.27	2.27
Bricklayers and masons	6,810	3,257	270	350	3.96	10.75
Carpenters	10,350	6,660	60	122	.58	1.83
Electricians	9,600	8,750	90	79	.94	.90
Machinists and toolmakers	14,940	14,606	60	245	.40	1.68
Mechanics (except auto)	6,810	3,721	270	62	3.96	1.67
Plumbers and pipefitters	11,310	8,687	120	62	1.06	.71
Building trades (not elsewhere classified)	3,900	2,791	180	207	4.62	7.42
Metal working trades	7,470	5,706	150	141	2.01	2.47
Printing trades	14,490	11,722	270	206	1.86	1.76
Other specified	12,210	8,905	480	386	3.93	4.33
Trade not specified	13,890	10,400	120	291	.86	2.80

SOURCE: Bureau of the Census, *U.S. Census of Population, 1950*, Vol. IV, Special Reports, Part I, Chapter B, "Occupational Characteristics" (Washington, D.C.: Government Printing Office, 1956) and *U.S. Census of Population, 1960*, "Occupational Characteristics," p. 26.

against any member who discriminates against a fellow member because of race.

A 1966 survey in Houston revealed no Negroes in the following unions: IBEW Local 716; Painters and Glaziers Local 130; Pipefitters Local 211; Sheet Metal Workers Local 54; Lathers Local 224; Bricklayers Local 7; Ironworkers Local 84. Carpenters Local 213, with 2,900 members, Plumbers Local 68, with 600 members, and Plasterers Local 79, with 170 members, each had 1 Negro member. The absence of Negroes from the Houston Bricklayers' local is an exception to that union's general practices in the South, where there have been many Negro members in integrated and segregated locals.

In a suit filed in February 1966, the United States Department of Justice alleged that the St. Louis Building and Construction Trades Council and several of its affiliates had violated Title VII of the Civil Rights Act of 1964 and were tortiously interfering with a nondiscrimination agreement between the United States and a contractor. Action was brought against the unions after their members walked off the job to protest the hiring of a Negro plumbing contractor and his employees, who were represented by the Congress of Industrial Unions, an integrated union not affiliated with the AFL-CIO. The unions offered to take all CIU members who were qualified, and argued that their strike was against the hiring of substandard workers and not because of race. However, the Justice Department alleged that the walkout, which shut down the project, was staged "to prevent and discourage the employment on construction projects in the St. Louis area of plumbers who are members of nondiscriminating unions." The Justice Department brief alleges that: Pipefitters Local 562 had over 1,000 members, none of whom is a Negro; Sheet Metal Workers Local 36 had 1,250 members, of whom only 2 apprentices were Negro; International Brotherhood of Electrical Workers Local 1 had 1,963 members only one of whom was a Negro; and Plumbers Local No. 35 had 1,200 members and 102 apprentices, none of whom were Negroes. The Justice

Department asked for injunctions to prevent these unions from frustrating the contractors' nondiscrimination clause in their Federal contracts and to prevent the unions from discriminating against any member or potential member.

Table 5.2, taken from a survey by the Mayor's Commission on Human Relations in Pittsburgh, shows the following unions to have had no nonwhite members: Asbestos Workers Local 2; Boilermakers Local 154; Plumbers Local 27; Sign Painters Local 479; Steamfitters Local 449; Stone and Marble Masons Local 33; Tile Setters Local 26; Elevator Constructors Local 6; Terrazzo Helpers Local 64; Plumbers Laborers Local 347; and Marble Polishers & Helpers Local 15. Most Negroes in the Pittsburgh building trades were in the Bricklayers (10–12 out of a total of 979), Carpenters (50 out of 7,500), Cement Masons (35–40 out of 748), Operating Engineers (120 out of 5,880), Lathers (14 out of 180), Painters (22 out of 800), and Sheet Metal Workers (20 out of 1,200). The Pittsburgh Iron Workers had 2 Negro members out of a 1,937 total, the IBEW had 1 out of 1,000, the Plasterers had 5 out of 254, and the Roofers—4 out of 186.

Following years of effort, IBEW Local 38 in Cleveland accepted its first 3 Negro journeymen in 1957, and this as a result of AFL-CIO President George Meany's threat to revoke the local's charter. In 1966, IBEW Local 38 still had only 2 Negro journeymen and 2 Negro apprentices among its 1,250 members. Plumbers in Cleveland had accepted 5 journeymen and 1 apprentice, the Iron Workers had 1 apprentice, and the Sheet Metal Workers had 1 Negro apprentice out of 1,400 members.

In 1966 the Ohio Civil Rights Commission released a report in which it stated that there were no Negro members in the Cincinnati Pipefitters, Plumbers, and Electricians unions which operated exclusive hiring hall arrangements with contractors. The Civil Rights Commission concluded that "There is a pattern of racial discrimination in the building trades industry in Cincinnati." The Commission concluded that discrimination was discernible among contractors, unions, and joint apprenticeship programs. It

TABLE 5.2
Nonwhite Participation in the Building
Trades Unions in the Pittsburgh Area Since July 8, 1963

UNION	TOTAL MEMBERS	TOTAL NONWHITES	CURRENT NUMBER OF APPRENTICES	NONWHITE APPRENTICE ADMISSIONS
Asbestos Workers Local 2	212	0	27	0
Boilermakers Local 154	610	0	12	0
Bricklayers Local 2	979	10–12*	32	0
Bridge and Iron Workers Local 3	1,937	2	1	0
Carpenters District Council of Pittsburgh and vicinity	7,500*	50*	115	3
Cement Masons Local 526	748	35–40*	15	3
International Brotherhood of Electrical Workers Local 5	1,000*	1	18*	0
Engineers Local 66	5,880	120*	19	0
Lathers Local 33	180	14	15	1
Painters Local 6	800*	22	22	1
Plasterers Local 31	254	5	6	1
Plumbers Local 27 ‡	886	0	27	—†

Roofers Local 37	186	4	10*	0
Sign Painters Local 479	147	0	6	0
Sheet Metal Workers Local 12	1,200	20*	50	2
Steamfitters Local 449	1,400*	0	50*	0
Stone and Marble Masons Local 33	238	0	5	0
Tile Setters Local 26	79	0	1	0
Construction General Laborers Local 373	2,500*	1,300*	—†	—†
Elevator Constructors Local 6	227	0	0	0
Glaziers Local 751	185	1	—†	—†
Terrazzo Helpers Local 64	33	0	—†	—†
Tile Layers and Helpers Local 20	68	4	—†	—†
Teamsters Local 341	1,225	350*	—†	—†
Plumbers Laborers Local 347	240	0	—†	—†
Marble Polishers and Helpers Local 15	30*	0	—**	—**

* Approximate figures.

† No apprentice program.

‡ Plumbers Local 27 was not surveyed, as the commission has been in litigation with this union since October 29, 1963. Figures are based upon the testimony of the local's officials in public hearings held November 27, 1963 and January 2 and 3, 1964.

** Number unknown.

SOURCE: *Status of Negroes in Craft Unions* (Pittsburgh: The Mayor's Commission on Human Relations, 1965).

alleged that unions practiced discrimination through job control, high and impractical admission standards, and "other discouraging devices."

An investigation of the New York building industry by the Commission on Human Rights (CHR) during 1963 disclosed "a pattern of exclusion in a substantial portion of the building and construction industry which effectively bars nonwhites from participating in this area of the city's economic life." [16] The CHR placed responsibility for this discrimination on employers, who "turned over the right to hire to others, notably to the trade unions under collective bargaining agreements with builders," and the unions, which imposed "almost insurmountable barriers" to nonwhites seeking union membership in a substantial number of the construction trades unions." [17] The commission noted that "whenever the employer had control over hiring, some nonwhites were employed. But in those trades where contractors traditionally relied upon the locals for referrals, nonwhites were effectively excluded from construction trades employment." Nonwhite journeymen were found by the CHR to face the union barriers of sponsorship requirements, discrimination in referrals, and priority given to out-of-town workers. Apprentices faced obstacles in the historical "for white only" clauses, "father-son" clauses, sponsorship requirements, and withholding of apprenticeship-journeyman ratios.

The 1963 CHR survey disclosed very few nonwhites in New York building trades locals, except for the Carpenters, who had 5,000 Negroes in a total membership of 34,000. None of the 4,000 Construction Steamfitters, 3,300 Sheet Metal Workers, or 3,000 Construction Plumbers were Negroes. The Elevator Constructors had "maybe" 3 Negro members. IBEW Local 3 in New York has been a clear exception to the general exclusionary practices of IBEW locals. Local 3 had graduated no Negro apprentices before 1961, but recruited 240 Negroes among 900 apprentices recruited in 1962. Local 3's action was taken at a time when it had agreed to take in more apprentices as a condition to negotiating for the 25-hour week. Its acceptance of the nonwhite apprentices undoubtedly made the IBEW's unpopular demand for a 25-hour week more palatable to New York City officials.

Although there were very few Negro members of craft locals in New York in 1963, between 1963 and 1965 building trades unions in that city took in a relatively large number of nonwhites. As a result of legal action by the New York State Commission for Human Rights, Sheet Metal Workers Local 28 of New York accepted a Negro into its apprenticeship program in the spring of 1965 for the first time and 14 nonwhites passed a test given the following November. However, no decision had been reached concerning the number of apprentices to be admitted to Local 28's program. The union had appealed an earlier order requiring it to accept 65 apprentices. Efforts to get Negroes and Puerto Ricans into New York building trades unions were intensified during 1963 as a result of demonstrations against several construction projects. In March 1965, the New York Building and Construction Trades Council reported that some 2,916 nonwhites, mostly Negroes, had been admitted to various unions in that city during 1963 and 1964. As Table 5.3 shows, 1,140 of these nonwhites were apprentices and 1,776 were journeymen. However, of the total, 1,600 were in the Carpenters and 319 in the Bricklayers. The IBEW was next with 240. The significance of the New York experience of admitting 1,140 nonwhite apprentices in 1963 and 1964 may be judged by the fact that 1960 census figures—which probably are inaccurate—reported in Table 5.1, show only 2,191 Negro apprentices in the United States. Peter J. Brennen, President of the Greater New York Building and Construction Trades Council, reported in a radio interview on May 29, 1966, that incomplete reports from BCTC members locals showed the construction unions to have taken in at least 286 apprentices and 515 journeymen from minority groups since March 1965.

ELECTRICIANS

No union has been more vigorously attacked for racial discrimination in recent years than the locals of the International Brotherhood of Electrical Workers (IBEW). One

TABLE 5.3

Partial Report on the Number of Nonwhites* Taken into the Various Building and Construction Trades Unions in the City of New York, March 1963–March 1965

UNION	NONWHITES	APPRENTICES †	JOURNEYMEN
Bricklayers Executive Council	319	52	267
Carpenters District Council	1,600	623	977
Operating Engineers Local 15	62	7	55
Operating Engineers Local 94	80	50	30
Electrical Workers Local 3	240	240	—
Decorative Glass Workers Local 520	4	4	—
Glass Warehouse Workers Local 206	102	—	102
Glaziers Local 1087	20	12	8
Ironworkers Local 361	8	8	—
Concrete Workers D.C.	37	—	37
General Building Laborers Local 51	23	—	23

Excavators Local 731	88	—	88
Plasterers Tenders Local 56	2	—	2
Painters District Council	105	30	75
Structural Steel Painters Local 806	14	3	11
Plumbers Local 1	30	16	14
Plumbers Local 2	19	9	10
Composition Roofers Local 8	18	2	16
Sheet Metal Workers Local 28†	—	—	—
Steamfitters Local 638	9	9	—
Window Cleaners Local 2	136	75	61
Total	2,916	1,140	1,776

* This does not include those who were given the opportunity and turned it down—those who were in and dropped out on their own volition and nonwhites who were in the union before March 1963.

† Apprenticeship classes started March 15, 1964.

SOURCE: Building and Construction Trades Council, New York City.

of the reasons for these attacks is that the electricians have high-paying jobs in an expanding industry and yet have had very few Negro members in construction locals. Although the IBEW did not have a racial bar in its constitution, it made no secret of its opposition to Negro members. In 1903, for example, the editor of the IBEW journal wrote: "We do not want the Negro in the International Brotherhood of Electrical Workers, but we think they should be organized in locals of their own affiliated with the American Federation of Labor, as the organization knows no creed or color." [18]

However, because Negroes were able to work as electricians, the IBEW's international officers were not satisfied with the practice of exclusion by local members. In 1905, therefore, the international sought to follow the common practice of organizing Negroes into auxiliary locals. But the organizer hired for this purpose soon resigned, complaining that Negroes refused to join auxiliary locals because other building trades unions gave them full rights.[19] The IBEW then decided to permit Negro locals to affiliate directly with the international if the white local in the area gave its consent.[20] But, very few local unions gave their consent, and except for a few locals in Chicago, New York, and Los Angeles, the IBEW had very few Negro members before the 1960's.

There was, however, a continuing conflict over this point between international IBEW leaders and the local unions. For example, IBEW international president J. P. Noonan urged the 1927 convention to organize Negro electricians. Noonan reported that the international had "at least one organization maintained by Negro wiremen, appealing to the AFL for a charter on the grounds that the IBEW will not organize them into locals already organized or issue a charter to them as a local union." [21] President Noonan denied that the admission of Negroes would imply social equality, arguing that organizing Negro competitors was an economic and not a social question. Moreover, he did not feel that organizing Negroes would result in the union being flooded with Negro electricians, a major fear of his members. Noonan felt that it was inconsistent to argue that the Negro was not a competent worker but that his competition threatened union standards.

Although IBEW construction locals rarely accepted Negroes, they sometimes permitted Negro contractors to work if they confined their operations to Negro neighborhoods. Indeed, IBEW locals have actually picketed Negro electricians when they tried to work outside the areas restricted to them, even though those locals adamantly refused to admit Negroes to membership. IBEW locals are able to enforce their rules against Negroes because they control the supply of skilled electricians and because other skilled union members refuse to work with nonunion men. Since electricians usually must be licensed, the unions sometimes strengthen their grip on the supply of labor by controlling the licensing boards. Although IBEW construction locals that accepted Negroes to membership before 1950 were the exception, subsequent legal action and pressures from the AFL-CIO and the international unions have forced locals in Washington, D.C., Hartford (Connecticut), Detroit, and Cleveland to accept Negro members.

The IBEW affiliate which has done the most to admit Negroes has been Local 3 in New York, which had only 8 Negroes in construction work in 1961, but which recruited 1,000 new apprentices in 1962, 240 of whom were Negro and 60 Puerto Rican. However, in 1965, except for New York, Chicago, and Los Angeles, few Northern IBEW construction locals had as many as 10 Negro members. And there probably were not 10 Negro members of IBEW construction locals in the entire South.

Connecticut adopted an approach to IBEW Local 35 in Hartford that was effective in getting Negroes admitted. The first case submitted to a public hearing before the Connecticut Civil Rights Commission (CCRC) involved Local 35's refusal to admit qualified Negroes to membership. Local 35 argued that it had not violated the law because it discriminated against all races! The Civil Rights Commission was not impressed by the union's argument, however, and ordered it to admit the Negroes. Yet the union defied both the CCRC and the force of public opinion by voting to reject the Negro applicants, despite a court order to accept them. Local 35 quickly capitulated, however, when it was fined $2,000 and $500 for each week it remained in contempt of court.[22]

PLUMBERS

The Plumbers' racial practices closely parallel those of the IBEW locals. Both organizations have successfully used licensing and inspection arrangements to restrict entry into their crafts. A 1958 survey by the National Urban League found that Plumbers locals had no Negroes in twenty of the twenty-three cities surveyed and the others had only token Negro membership. The following are typical comments from various cities concerning the plumbers' racial practices:

Akron, Ohio: "Because there are no Negro members in the union and because we know of Negroes having been refused journeyman and apprenticeship status, we consider the practices of the union unfavorable."

Cincinnati, Ohio: "The plumbers are exclusively all (with negligible exceptions) white. Since there are a fair number of Negroes doing the skilled jobs for non-union contracting firms, and since many union contractors accept Negroes for the common labor jobs, it seems unlikely that all union contractors adamantly refuse to hire Negroes for any skilled classification. It seems more reasonable to assume that the Plumbers union has consciously and systematically excluded Negroes."

Columbus, Ohio: "Negroes are excluded from membership. The transfer cards of Negroes coming into the Columbus area are not honored. Apprenticeship programs not open to Negroes."

Tampa, Florida: "Strongly anti-Negro throughout the South. No Negro membership likely unless change in policy."

San Francisco, California: "Outstanding resistance by some unions have made it virtually impossible to place Negroes in certain categories of craft union skill. The Plumbers Union is one of the worst offenders."

Pittsburgh, Pennsylvania: "No Negro membership. There are approximately 20 Negro journeymen plumbers in Pittsburgh who work primarily for small Negro contractors."

Portland, Oregon: "Since the passage of the Oregon State law against discrimination and the filing of complaints against some of the unions, there has been a relaxing of resistance to minority membership. However, some are still persistently trying to evade the law, particularly the Plumbers and Pipefitters."

As with many IBEW locals, legal action has revealed a clear and unmistakable pattern of discrimination. The Steamfitters, for example, had 1,400 members in Pittsburgh in 1963 and the Plumbers had 886 members, but neither had a single Negro member. In a 1965 Pittsburgh case UA Local 27 was found guilty in county court of having discriminated against 2 Negro applicants by barring them from membership while taking in whites.

There have, however, been some significant breakthroughs in Plumbers locals. One of these occurred in Cleveland, where civil rights groups conducted demonstrations against the Plumbers and other building trades unions. After lengthy negotiations, a 1963 Cleveland dispute was settled by an agreement between civil rights representatives, Plumbers Local 55 officials, company representatives, officials of the city of Cleveland, John F. Henning, then Under Secretary of Labor, and Donald Slaiman, Director of the AFL-CIO's Civil Rights Department. Under this settlement, Local 55 agreed to accept Negro plumbing contractors and their journeymen employees and apprentices who passed a test. The agreement also provided for review of journeymen examinations by a committee comprised of representatives of the union, the United States Department of Labor, and civil rights organizations. On August 15, 1963, Local 55 admitted a Negro contractor with his 4 journeymen and 2 apprentices; in December,

1965, Local 55 had 5 Negro journeymen and 1 Negro apprentice.

INTERNATIONAL AND NATIONAL UNIONS

For understandable reasons, there is an important distinction between the policies of national or international * and local unions. International unions gain power and prestige from expansion, whereas local craft unions often maintain the wage and employment conditions of their members by restricting membership. National unions also are more conspicuous and therefore more vulnerable to moral pressures. Although their locals are notorious for discriminating, both the UA and the IBEW have become concerned about the adverse publicity they have received. The UA established a committee in 1959 to study charges of racial discrimination against its locals and in 1962 the international union included a nondiscrimination clause in its national agreement covering large contractors. The UA's international president, Peter Schoemann, told his members, in a widely publicized statement: "The fact is, we have a problem. Despite significant actions taken in some locals, this problem in too many cases has not yet been solved, and the sands of time are running out." Schoemann told his members that the solution to the Negro problem was "take them in."

But, critics ask, if internationals are sincere in their nondiscrimination policies, why do they not force their locals to admit Negroes? Union leaders reply that they cannot do this because their locals are autonomous— reasoning which is not entirely convincing because internationals have varying degrees of power over their locals. As a general rule, the international's control over its local affiliates is determined by such factors as the nature of the market, the political situation within the union, the size and importance of the locals involved, provisions in the international constitution relating to the ownership of property,

* Unions are called "international" if they have locals outside the United States. In this book these terms are used interchangeably.

and the ease of establishing trusteeships over the local by the international. The nature of the market is a particularly important distinction between industrial and building trades locals because the localized nature of the construction industry gives the building trades locals considerable autonomy. Industrial locals are often less autonomous because nationwide markets require national coordination in collective bargaining.

Although the principle of local autonomy has been a very real factor in the American labor movement, the problem of racial discrimination would seem to place a strong responsibility on the internationals to compel compliance with state and Federal laws and with union policy. Indeed, within the labor movement the international alone has the necessary power to change the ways of discriminating locals. It would be unrealistic to expect local elected officers to deal with the problem because they risk being defeated for office if they take unpopular actions.

The internationals' usual powers over local unions have been strengthened by the passage of the 1964 Civil Rights Act, the strengthening of the Federal antidiscrimination provisions in government contracts, antidiscrimination standards in apprenticeship training programs, NLRB decisions making racial discrimination an unfair labor practice, and the state antidiscrimination laws. If the internationals are unable to persuade their local members that racial equality is good trade unionism, they should be able to convince them that they will most likely face prosecution and will bring embarrassment to the whole labor movement as well as to the locals involved. The internationals would perform a much needed service to both themselves and the labor movement if they used trusteeships and other measures necessary to eliminate discrimination.

SUMMARY

The evidence seems to support the following conclusions concerning unions which bar Negroes from membership by informal means:

Racial exclusion by informal means is not restricted

to any particular geographic area. Though restriction is undoubtedly more rigid in the South, there are some unions that have relatively more Negro members in the South than elsewhere: the trowel trades, Longshoremen, Teamsters, Roofers, and Hod Carriers and Common Laborers. These trades have been practiced by Negroes in the South because they have been regarded as "Negro work" and because Negroes have sufficient supplies of labor to protect their interests and to protect employers who might be boycotted by whites. These occupations also have relatively old and stable techniques, making it difficult for unions to exclude Negroes by monopolizing the latest technology.

Although some of the craft unions have had equalitarian racial policies while some industrial unions have refused to admit Negroes, as a general rule the unions which practice exclusion are craft organizations. Craft locals can exclude Negroes from membership and from the trade if they can control the labor supply. Industrial unions, on the other hand, organize workers after they are hired. In addition, craft unions at the local level consider it to their advantage to exclude workers, while industrial unions consider it to their advantage to organize extensively.

These factors are not sufficient, however, to explain the practice of exclusion. Other relevant considerations include the following: because of the developing equalitarian trend in race relations, older unions seem more likely to exclude minorities than new unions; in many cases the employer determines the hiring policy and therefore decides whether Negroes are to be hired; Negroes are likely to be excluded from jobs like plumbing, milk delivering, and electrical work, which require home deliveries or repairs; whites are likely to attempt to exclude Negroes from certain status jobs; and, in some cases, exclusion is directed against all except a particular nationality group —it has been common practice in the building trades and some garment unions, for instance, for locals to be restricted to a particular nationality group.

While the foregoing evidence suggests widespread racial discrimination, it should be emphasized that, in the case of the building trades unions, racial restrictions are not due entirely to racial reasons. Craft unionists are likely to have strong feelings of property rights in their crafts and their unions. They believe that these property rights have been won through years of training and fighting to build and strengthen unions. Any encroachment on either their jobs or their traditional union practices is likely to be resented—whether the encroachment comes from the international union, governments, or civil rights organizations. There is a pervasive belief among building trades unionists that civil rights groups want special treatment for Negroes at the expense of the unions' members. This belief combines with strong depression-created fears of unemployment, and these fears, in turn, are reinforced by the casual nature of the construction industry. In short, much of what appears to be discrimination by building trades unions is in reality resentment at outside pressures. In these circumstances, while discrimination is obviously also a factor, union members are less likely to be motivated by racial prejudices than determination to win the contest against outside interference.

Auxiliary and Segregated Locals

As has been noted, a number of international unions have restricted Negroes to auxiliary locals, an arrangement that was usually adopted in lieu of formal exclusion and was sometimes the next stage following the elimination of formal restrictions. An intermediate stage between outright exclusion and auxiliary locals frequently was the organization of federal locals for Negroes, as illustrated by the IAM, the BRSC, and the Boilermakers. Sometimes, however, this intermediate stage was skipped altogether and auxiliaries were fused with exclusion. A few auxiliaries remained in 1959, but they had become relatively unimportant by that date. The difference between segregated locals and auxiliaries is that the segregated locals have equal status with white locals and separate charters, but this distinction is often more theoretical than real, because the whites might in fact bargain for the Negro locals.

Locals sometimes are referred to as "segregated" when in fact they have mixed memberships. In cities with large Negro populations, building trades locals were established in Negro areas, but many of these later took in some white members. This pattern was followed by locals of the Carpenters, International Longshoremen's Association, Bricklayers, Musicians, Hod Carriers and Common Laborers, and Painters. In Washington, D.C., for example, the previously segregated Negro Bricklayers local had about 10 percent white membership in 1962 and the "white" local had about 20 percent Negroes. Sometimes the locals were in occupations—like hod carriers and common laborers—which were traditionally "Negro" jobs which whites moved into during depressions or when wages or working conditions in those occupations improved. Of course, in many places some jobs are held almost exclusively by Negroes, so the unions also tend to be all-Negro.

Segregated locals have existed throughout the country, but most of them have been in the South; in some cases segregation was insisted upon by the Negroes as a condition for joining. Segregation also was imposed because of local laws against integrated meetings, and even where there have been no segregation laws, community pressures frequently required segregation. Indeed, about the only union with a long history in the South which did not establish segregated locals was the United Mine Workers, whose members were isolated and relatively impervious to community pressure. Even so, seating in UMW locals often was segregated (and in some cases in Alabama remained segregated as late as 1965) and the Miners were frequently attacked in the South because of their integrated meetings.

Actually, there were relatively few segregated locals in 1966, that is, separate unions in the same plant or craft, although a few unions almost invariably were segregated in the South—the Carpenters, the Longshoremen, the Paper Makers, the Pulp Sulphite Workers, the Brotherhood of Railway Clerks, the Tobacco Workers, and the

Musicians. But CIO international unions rarely had more than two or three segregated locals. Even unions like the Tobacco Workers, with predominantly Southern memberships, adopted a policy after 1946 of not forming new segregated locals. Other unions, such as the Bricklayers, have a relatively small number of segregated locals in the South. Thus, only 25 of the Bricklayers' 168 Southern locals were segregated in 1960.

Segregated local unions have encountered increasing opposition from Negro and civil rights groups since World War II. The Negro community is convinced that segregation in unions, like other forms of segregation, contributes to the Negro's economic disadvantages and should therefore be abolished. Consequently, those Negro union leaders who favored segregation as a means of preserving the advantages of union leadership and of affording Negroes some control over their own affairs find themselves out of harmony with the mainstream of Negro opinion.

White reactions to integration are not always predictable but a key factor seems to be the proportion of Negro to white members in the locals: whites usually have resisted integration when they would be in the minority in the merged organizations. White opposition also will be great either where whites expect to lose their relative seniority positions in integrated rosters, or where Negroes will acquire previously all-white jobs. This, for example, was a problem in the tobacco, aircraft, and paper industries in the South when the Federal Government forced the integration of seniority rosters and local unions. Finally, where groups like the Ku Klux Klan or White Citizens Councils raise the issue, white members are likely to resist integration—at least publicly.

Some of the problems that result from merging locals affect Negroes and whites alike. The attitudes of Negro and white rank-and-file members are likely to be shaped, for example, by their interpretation of the economic advantages and disadvantages of integration. In some occupations (longshoremen, bricklayers, and musicians in the South) Negroes feel that their economic conditions will not be improved by integration. Indeed, there is even some apprehension that Negro job opportunities might actually deteriorate if integration destroys protected markets. Initially, the most successful mergers of Musicians, Longshoremen, Tobacco Workers, and Machinists seem to have required that Negroes, who were usually in a minority, be given some official positions in the merged organizations. While such special treatment for Negroes signifies that the groups really are not "integrated," some union officials consider these to be important first steps toward integration. That these arrangements are considered temporary is suggested by the fact that they are rarely formalized or stated as official policy.

These general propositions can be illustrated by the experiences of several international unions.

INTERNATIONAL LONGSHOREMEN'S ASSOCIATION

In the South, International Longshoremen's Association (ILA) locals have maintained rigid systems of job and union segregation, and Negroes frequently complain of complete exclusion from sections of New York, Philadelphia, Boston, and other Northern piers. On the Gulf ports, there are segregated general longshoremen's locals, and share-the-work agreements have controlled job allocations since the Civil War. In the South and outside of it, the better clerks and checkers jobs usually are controlled by whites, whose locals almost invariably have barred Negroes from membership. Negroes have retained their general longshore jobs on Southern docks partly because Negro longshoremen provide dependable supplies of labor in this sometimes heavy, uncertain, and disagreeable work, partly because employers say Negroes are "better suited" than whites for some longshoring jobs, and partly because even the most prejudiced hiring agents are afraid to discriminate against Negroes because discriminating employers can easily be boycotted.

In exchange for the racial job-sharing arrangements, Negro leaders have supported the ILA in bargaining with employers and against the organizing efforts of the International Longshoremen and Warehousemen's Union. These mutually beneficial arrangements have produced some powerful Negro ILA leaders and for years Negro vice-presidents from the South have held important positions in the ILA's power structure. Such Negro leaders naturally are likely to resist any changes that threaten their positions.

The ILA's racial division of labor may be illustrated by the composition of that union's New Orleans membership. In 1962, there were approximately 7,000 ILA members in New Orleans—1,900 whites and 5,100 Negroes. Each race controlled four locals, all of which were represented in a joint council, and all locals had concurrent jurisdiction except for 375 white clerks and checkers and 1,200 Negro freight-car unloaders. A management representative told the writer in 1965 that whites were "losing out" on the New Orleans docks; the crews are referred out on the basis of productivity, and the Negroes were more productive.

BUILDING TRADES

The Negro bricklayers, plasterers, cement finishers, and roofers are usually integrated in the South. Negro workers have been able to retain these jobs because they have sufficiently large supplies of labor to furnish the entire requirements of contractors who might be boycotted by whites. Indeed, these workers, like the longshoremen, frequently have better employment opportunities in the South than outside of it, where they are discriminated against by white unions in some cases. The Bricklayers had about twenty-five segregated locals in the South in 1962, but they were also integrated in some places. It has been common practice for some unions with all-Negro or virtually all-Negro membership to have white officers as "contact" men in situations where employers refuse to deal with Negro officers.

Except for the so-called "trowel trades," however, Negro building trades workers often have been unhappy with segregation because they have inadequate job opportunities. For example, several Negro locals of the

United Brotherhood of Carpenters and Joiners (UBCJ) in the South have virtually atrophied because they could not get adequate job opportunities. In many Southern cities Negro carpenters locals have survived in some cases by insisting upon quota systems on Federal projects. In other cases, the small Negro locals are restricted to house work in the Negro sections and the business agents sometimes act as contractors.

The UBCJ announced in 1963 that segregated locals and other forms of racial discrimination would be abolished in that union, and in March 1964, a UBCJ official told the writer that "in the past three years some eleven segregated Local Unions have been merged or disbanded." [23] Other Carpenters' locals have subsequently been merged. One of the most important of these was at New Orleans where a merger was accomplished in 1965. Moreover, surveys during 1965 indicated that the Carpenters were actively seeking Negro apprentices in many cities. With respect to the economic effects of segregation, the UBCJ's general treasurer, who handles all matters pertaining to discrimination for the Carpenters' Executive Board, explained:

> . . . both whites and colored have suffered. The Negroes suffered because they lacked the strength and perhaps the know-how to make gains they might be entitled to. But the whites have been held back even more, because they have had a low-wage competitive factor working against them. In spite of Hell or high water, the lowest wages form the lowest common denominator that affects all wages. This is the main reason why we oppose segregation in any form.[24]

AMERICAN FEDERATION OF MUSICIANS

As late as 1960, the American Federation of Musicians (AFM) probably had more segregated locals scattered throughout the United States than any union except the Railway Clerks. Like other unions, discussed above, the AFM at first organized Negroes into auxiliary locals. When James C. Petrillo became president of the AFM in 1940, he granted equal status to the twelve remaining Negro auxiliaries. Many locals continued to be segregated, however, because Petrillo had a policy of creating separate locals when fifty Negroes "requested their own charter and could meet the charter requirements." [25]

After World War II increasing Negro opposition to segregation caused a policy change. Sometimes Negro opposition stemmed from inadequate job opportunities, especially work with symphony orchestras, but the greatest opposition within the AFM seems to have come from a few Negro leaders who opposed segregation on principle. Leadership for this opposition was provided by a Los Angeles Negro local, which merged with a white local in 1953 after the Negroes threatened a lawsuit. Negro representatives from this local also introduced a resolution at the 1957 AFM convention calling for the elimination of segregated locals.

The vast majority of Negro delegates to the 1957 convention opposed this antisegregation resolution. Fifty-seven delegates from 39 of the federation's 47 Negro locals presented a petition opposing the merger resolution because "of the financial aspect involved with some of the larger colored locals, who have spent many years of hard work to attain their present status in the Federation. . . . Under no circumstances should a merger be forced upon us but should rather be accomplished by mutual agreement between parties concerned." [26] Only 4 Negro delegates from 2 locals opposed this petition. After the 1957 convention, Petrillo had all members of the AFM's Negro locals vote on the merger resolution. Of the locals, 40 voted against merger, 5 in favor of it, and 2 did not vote.[27] But, the matter was not settled by the 1957 convention because the AFM's policies were subjected to increasing external pressures. The Los Angeles Negroes filed a complaint against the AFM with the AFL-CIO Civil Rights Committee in 1958.

Herman Kenin, Petrillo's successor as president of the AFM, at first continued Petrillo's policies. However, the passage of state antidiscrimination legislation and the changing national racial climate, especially after 1962, apparently caused the federation to assign greater urgency to the problem of eliminating segregated locals. According to Mr. Kenin, "A changing national climate . . . is aiding us somewhat in the tedious, difficult and time-consuming procedures that become necessary to the protection of job and property rights of merged minorities." [28] By the end of 1962, the federation had merged all of its locals west of Omaha, and in 1963 delivered an ultimatum to its Chicago affiliates to merge by March 1, 1964. Previously, however, some 50 Negroes had joined the white local in Chicago because of the refusal of their local to merge. In March 1965, the AFM had about 30 all-Negro locals, but a number of these were subsequently merged and the AFM reported that it was moving toward "total integration."

While the number of segregated locals is declining, they are not likely to disappear completely for many years. Several international unions, like the Machinists, the Bricklayers, Longshoremen, Paper Makers, and various railroad unions, have policies encouraging merger but, respecting local autonomy, apparently will not employ sanctions to enforce mergers. Moreover, although segregation violates the Civil Rights Act of 1964, Negro opposition to the merger of some locals ensures that Negro locals probably will continue to maintain their identity. Those Negroes who object to segregation probably will join white locals. If the latter accept Negro members and if interunion transfers are voluntary, there probably will be few objections to the continuation of predominantly Negro or white locals.

The most important forces tending to eliminate segregated locals have been: prevailing moral sentiment against segregation, opposition from the Negro community (as contrasted with Negro union members), some state FEP laws, and the Kennedy and Johnson administrations' policy of not permitting segregated locals to bargain for government employees and of strongly discouraging their use by Federal contractors. Moreover, almost all international unions have signed pledges with the President's Committee on Equal Employment Opportunity agreeing to abolish discrimination, including segregated locals, within their unions.

Conclusions

This chapter has shown that the racial practices of national and local unions have varied considerably according to time, place, and circumstance. The most obvious change in these practices brought about by time has been the decline in the number of national unions with formal race bars in their constitutions; there also has been a significant change in the practice of establishing auxiliary and segregated local unions. Indeed, it seems reasonable to conclude that the problems of formal exclusion and segregation had become relatively unimportant by 1966. Informal exclusion by some craft unions, especially in the building trades, had become the central problem in discrimination. The elimination of segregated seniority rosters, discussed in the following chapter, was also an important step in the South. Because the entry of Negroes into apprenticeship training programs is determined by numerous factors in addition to discrimination, and because the building trades unions are strong enough to exercise considerable control over entry into their trades, the upgrading of Negroes in this industry is likely to be a source of friction between unions and the Negro community for some time.

Within the labor movement the main problem of discrimination is at the local level. The AFL-CIO has adopted a strong antidiscrimination policy and seems to be actively doing what it can to implement it. Unfortunately, the AFL-CIO has very limited power over the discriminating locals. And, within the local unions the leaders too often are afraid they will be voted out if they adopt nondiscrimination policies. Clearly, therefore, the internationals should bear the greatest responsibility for eradicating discrimination, because only they have sufficient power to accomplish this objective. The excuse of local autonomy should be no more permissible in cases of racial discrimination than it is where locals violate other trade union policies or Federal, state, and local laws, especially now that unions can point to the threat of increasing government regulation and severe damage to the entire labor movement unless they deal with this problem. It would also seem that the discrimination problem is now sufficiently critical for the internationals to recognize the need to eradicate the problem before crises develop. No agencies have the ability to learn as much about discrimination in local unions as do the international officers. It would seem to be better strategy for the internationals to proceed vigorously—through trusteeships if necessary—against the worst offenders than to let discriminating unions damage the whole labor movement.

In addition, local unions should be encouraged to take the following steps:

1. Make it clear to the Negro community that all qualified applicants will be accepted.

2. See to it that tests for journeymen and apprentices are realistic in terms of the requirements for the trades. Tests might be administered by outside organizations, as is already done in many cases.

3. Local unions might have printed material which clearly explains the qualifications for membership and apprenticeship training programs. Apprenticeship openings should be announced to various community relations organizations, civil rights organizations, and Negro community leaders.

4. Unions might also maintain channels of communications with Negro leaders in order to clear up misunderstandings.

5. Locals might also keep careful records which would be available for inspection to authorized persons.

6. Although not many unions with exclusionist traditions are likely to do so voluntarily, unions should adopt really affirmative nondiscrimination programs that would not passively process Negro applicants who show up, but would actively search out qualified Negroes for member-

ship as journeymen or apprentices. The unions could, in this way, more clearly determine the kinds of applicants they get rather than taking only those referred by civil rights groups.

Chapter VI

ECONOMIC CONDITIONS
OF NEGRO WORKERS

The pattern of segregation established in the South by 1900 extended to jobs as well as to other aspects of life. Since complete separation of the races obviously would have been very difficult in nonagricultural employment, job segregation was expressed more in terms of status than physical separation. In the building trades and on the railroads, where racism had its strongest manifestations, white engineers, electricians, and plumbers who barred Negroes from their occupations and their unions nevertheless worked in close proximity with Negro firemen, laborers, helpers, and masons. In the shop crafts, Negroes were restricted to helper classifications, even when they taught the trade to white craftsmen.

Negroes held some skilled and supervisory positions, but these were either in all-Negro shops or in traditional

"Negro" jobs; when jobs became mechanized, they were defined as white jobs. For example, when the locomotive firemen's job consisted of the hard, dirty work of shoveling coal into engines, it was regarded as "Negro" work, but when the automatic stoker made this job cleaner and easier, whites tried to displace Negroes. There also was an apparent tendency for whites to displace Negroes from certain low-status jobs, for example, as bellboys in hotels, during recessions. In factories, Negroes were rarely hired except in laborer and janitorial classifications. Although this system undoubtedly was more rigid in the South, the same basic pattern existed in the North. Indeed, in some trades Negroes actually had greater opportunities in the South than elsewhere.

These job patterns obviously tended both to reflect and to perpetuate the racial caste system. Restricting Negroes to inferior jobs strengthened the image of them as "inferior" people, and the low incomes associated with these jobs made it difficult for them to acquire the education, housing, and physical means necessary for participation in the mainstream of American life. Those Negroes who became educated and skilled were restricted to work in Negro neighborhoods, where work requirements and facilities were limited, even for the professions. Negro doctors were not permitted the advantages of practicing in the best hospitals or participating in local medical societies. Negro craftsmen could not fill the better jobs, and Negro teachers taught in inferior schools. This occupational caste system not only made it difficult for Negroes to work and develop to the limit of their capacities, but also cost the economy billions of dollars in lost productivity and wasted human resources. There is no way of knowing exactly how much the nation has lost from this system, but the President's Council of Economic Advisors has estimated that in 1962 the cost of discrimination was perhaps $13 billion.[1]

The statistical data available demonstrate some changes in racial employment patterns, but they also show remarkable rigidity through time.

The Patterns of Racial Employment

That nonwhites are gradually being upgraded into the white-collar and skilled-labor categories is shown in Table 6.1, but that they are still concentrated disproportionately in the less skilled and service occupations is also evident. In 1962, 47.2 percent of whites in the labor force were in the white-collar categories, compared with only 16.7 percent of nonwhites, and 14.7 percent of nonwhites and only 2.1 percent of whites were in the private household category.

In many ways, nonwhite females have better job opportunities than nonwhite males. In the professional and technical category, for example, nonwhite females were 4.6 percent of employed women in 1940 and 6.8 percent in 1962; the comparable figures for nonwhite males were 3.1 percent and 3.5 percent. Table 6.2 shows that nonwhite males increased their proportion relative to total male employment in every category between 1940 and 1944, but declined in every category except craftsmen, foremen, and kindred workers when the war was over. Although nonwhite males have never regained their wartime proportion of total male employment, they had regained their proportions of the craftsmen and white-collar categories by 1962.

FEDERAL EMPLOYMENT

Negroes have made significant improvement in their employment positions in the government service, as indicated by the following nonwhite proportions of all government employees between 1940 and 1962:

1940	5.6%
1956	9.7
1960	10.7
1961	11.4
1962	12.1

SOURCE: Department of Labor, *The Economic Situation of Negroes in the United States*, Bulletin S–3 (Washington, D.C.: Government Printing Office, 1962), p. 8.

TABLE 6.1
Occupational Distribution of
the Civilian Labor Force by Color, 1957, 1962, and Projections for 1972

OCCUPATION GROUP	1957		1962		1972	
	WHITE	NONWHITE	WHITE	NONWHITE	WHITE	NONWHITE
White-collar workers	43.9%	13.3%	47.2%	16.7%	53.4%	24.2%
Professional, technical	10.7	4.0	12.6	5.3	17.0	8.7
Managerial, props.	11.2	2.4	11.9	2.6	12.1	2.9
Clerical	15.1	5.5	15.8	7.2	16.8	10.4
Sales	6.9	1.4	6.9	1.6	7.5	2.2
Blue-collar workers	37.9	41.1	35.3	39.5	31.0	35.7
Craftsmen, foremen	14.3	5.4	13.6	6.0	12.9	7.3
Operatives	19.0	20.5	17.4	19.9	14.9	19.2
Laborers	4.6	15.2	4.3	13.6	3.2	9.2
Service workers	9.3	32.1	10.7	32.8	11.1	32.5
Private household	1.9	14.8	2.1	14.7	1.8	13.0
Other	7.4	17.3	8.6	18.1	9.3	19.5
Farmers	8.9	13.5	6.8	11.0	4.5	7.6
Total	100.0	100.0	100.0	100.0	100.0	100.0

SOURCE: Statement by Sidney Sonenblum of the Department of Labor to Senate Subcommittee on Manpower and Employment, *Hearings*, Part 5 (September 1963), p. 1400.

TABLE 6.2

Proportion of Nonwhite to Total Males in Each Occupational Group, 1940–1962*

OCCUPATION GROUP	1962	1959	1952	1950	1948	1944	1940
Total employed men	9.2%	9.2%	8.9%	8.3%	8.4%	9.8%	9.0%
Professional, technical, and kindred workers	3.5	3.0	2.5	2.6	2.6	3.3	3.1
Managers, officials and proprietors, except farm	2.5	1.5	1.6	1.9	1.8	2.1	1.5
Clerical, and kindred workers	8.1	6.5	3.4†	2.8†	2.3†	2.8†	1.6
Sales workers	2.5	1.8					1.4
Craftsmen, foremen, and kindred workers	4.4	4.2	4.0	3.9	3.7	3.6	2.7
Operatives and kindred workers	11.4	10.7	10.4	8.5	10.1	10.1	6.1
Private household	—	37.7	31.6	51.3	53.7	75.2	61.8
Service, except private household	20.7	20.6	21.7	21.4	20.7	21.9	17.4
Laborers, except farm and mine	27.6	29.5	26.9	21.4	23.6	27.6	21.2
Farmers and farm managers	8.5	8.2	10.7	10.5	9.8	11.0	13.1
Farm laborers and foremen	24.9	24.0	16.2	19.8	15.8	21.1	22.5

* April of selected years.   † Includes sales 1944–1952.

source: Bureau of the Census, as reported by Department of Labor, Bureau of Labor Statistics, *Negroes in the United States: Their Employment and Economic Status*, Bulletin No. 1119, 1952 and *The Economic Situation of Negroes in the United States*, Bulletin S–3, 1962.

Nevertheless, a 1961 survey of Federal employment by the President's Committee on Equal Employment Opportunity (PCEEO) revealed that although Negroes held 8.9 percent of the Classification Act or similar positions, 72 percent of their jobs were in the lower GS–1 through GS–4 classifications, with starting salaries between $3,185 and $4,985, whereas only 35 percent of all employees were in these low categories. Although 50 percent of all Federal employees were in the GS–5 through GS–11 classifications, with starting salaries ranging between $4,345 and $9,640, only 27 percent of Negroes were in these categories. And Negroes held only 1 percent of the GS–12 through GS–18 ($8,955 to $18,500) positions.[2]

Since this survey, however, there has been some further improvement in the Negro's position in the Federal service. Between 1961 and 1963 total Negro employment increased by 6.8 percent and the number of Negroes in the higher classifications increased much faster than the totals in those classifications. Between 1961 and 1962, the number of Negroes in GS–5 through GS–11 jobs increased by 19.2 percent as compared with a total increase of 2.4 percent, and Negroes in GS–12 through GS–18 jobs increased by 35.6 percent, while the total rose by only 9.5 percent. This trend has continued in subsequent years.[3] The Negro percentage increases look more impressive than the absolute numbers involved, however, because few Negroes are in the higher positions. Between 1962 and 1963, for example, the absolute increases in Negro employment were as follows:

GS–12 through GS–18	545
GS–5 through GS–11	4,278
Wage board jobs paying over $8,000	183

FEDERAL CONTRACTORS

The PCEEO's compliance review program also makes some information available concerning Negro employment by Federal contractors.[4] The 1962 survey found that Negroes held 6.3 percent of the 4.2 million jobs reported by some 10,000 Federal contractors, but only 1.3 percent of the white-collar jobs. Moreover, it was found that colleges and universities accounted for 49 percent of the 10,000 white-collar jobs held by Negro women and 30 percent of the 11,000 white-collar jobs held by Negro men. Although 34.5 percent of all male blue-collar workers were in the skilled categories, only 9.3 percent of Negro males were in these categories; 6.1 percent of white and 4.8 percent of Negro women were in the skilled categories.

The compliance review surveys indicate a minute improvement in the Negro's employment status since 1962. In 4,610 identical units filing reports in 1962 and 1963, Negroes increased their proportions as follows:

OCCUPATION GROUP	1962	1963
All occupations	6.4%	6.5%
White-collar	1.2	1.3
Blue-collar	9.7	9.8

Between 1962 and 1964 there were 4,200 identical reporting units, which reported 6.6 percent Negroes in 1962 and 6.7 percent in 1964. During this period total employment increased by 2.9 percent and Negro employment rose by 4.9 percent. Negroes held 1.4 percent of white-collar jobs in 1962 and 1.7 percent in 1964. Total white-collar employment increased by 8 percent between 1962 and 1964, and Negro white-collar employment rose by 30.9 percent.

The 1964 survey also revealed that Negro females had much better representation in white-collar categories than Negro males. For example, 1.6 percent of Negro males and 6 percent of Negro females were in the professional category, and 1 percent of Negro males and 6.9 percent of Negro females were in the technical categories. Negro males constituted 6.9 percent of total male employment in the 1964 reporting units, and Negro females constituted 6.2 percent of total female employment, but Negro females constituted 5.1 percent of female professionals and 9.7 percent of female technical employees. Negro males were 1 percent of male professionals and 2.1 percent of male technical employees.

INCOME AND LABOR FORCE PARTICIPATION RATES

The evidence suggests that much of the improvement in nonwhite occupational levels in the postwar period has been caused by migration from rural areas in the South and by other forces which also affect whites, and not because of significant changes in the factors influencing the Negro's job patterns themselves. Indeed, although there has been considerable improvement in the Negroes' relative family income position since 1939, their position relative to whites deteriorated in the 1950's and 1960's. The median nonwhite family income relative to whites reached a postwar high of 56.8 percent in 1952 but declined to 51.2 percent in 1958 and was only 53 percent in 1962. There has at the same time, however, been a rather steady improvement in the absolute income of nonwhites. In 1960, 49 percent of the nation's 4.3 million nonwhite families had annual incomes of $3,000 or less; in 1964, 39 percent of the 4.8 million nonwhite families remained in this category. The median wage or salary income of nonwhite males fourteen years of age or older who were employed full time increased from $639 a year in 1939 to $2,831 in 1955 and $3,799 in 1962. Relative to white males, these nonwhite incomes were 45 percent of whites in 1939, 64 percent in 1955, 67 percent at the relative postwar high in 1960, and 63 percent in 1962. The percentages of nonwhite to white males ranged from 61 percent to 67 percent in the 1955–62 period.

Not all of the factors responsible for these changes in relative income positions, however, are known. Clearly, the major causes of improvement in the Negroes' income have been their migration out of the rural South, declining racial barriers, better training, and improved education. The forces causing the deterioration in nonwhite incomes relative to whites during the 1950's and 1960's included the declining relative participation rates of nonwhite males (who have higher incomes than nonwhite women) and the nonwhites' higher rates of unemployment (again, with a worsening of the nonwhite male's relative position).

The civilian labor force participation rates in 1962 were 60 percent for nonwhites and 56.1 percent for whites, but the nonwhite male participation rate (76.4 percent) was *lower* than the white male rate (78.5 percent), while the nonwhite female rate (45.6 percent) was much higher than the white female rate (35.6 percent). The participation rates for both nonwhite males and females was higher in 1948 (84.8 percent and 44.4 percent) than the rates for whites (84.2 percent and 30.6 percent). Although the nonwhite and white female participation rates do not seem to follow this pattern, the disparity between the male participation rates seems to increase during periods of unemployment. The deterioration of the participation rate of nonwhite males relative to white males and nonwhite females undoubtedly is due in part to declining employment opportunities in many unskilled and semiskilled jobs where Negro males traditionally have been employed. There has at the same time been an increase in the demand for service workers, where nonwhite females have been employed. Nonwhite females and white males and females have had higher levels of education than nonwhite males, which is probably another important reason why nonwhite males have not been upgraded as rapidly as other groups.

In 1964, in spite of over twenty years of sustained agitation by civil rights groups, nearly half of all Negro men still worked in such service jobs as laborers, janitors, and busboys. Although they had made more progress than men, about 40 percent of Negro women were employed in domestic service. There was nevertheless a striking increase in the number of nonwhite women employed in the professional, clerical, and managerial sales categories; between 1960 and 1965, the proportion of nonwhite females in these categories rose from 18 to 24 percent.

THE PROBLEM OF UNEMPLOYMENT

The deterioration in the nonwhite employment picture after 1953 is indicated by the following unemployment rates:

YEAR	WHITE	NONWHITE
1947	3.3%	5.4%
1951	2.8	4.8
1952	2.4	4.6
1953	2.3	4.1
1954	4.5	8.9
1955	3.6	7.9
1956	3.3	7.5
1957	3.9	8.0
1958	6.1	12.6
1959	4.9	10.7
1960	5.0	10.2
1961	6.0	12.5
1962	4.9	11.0
1963	5.1	10.9
1964	4.6	9.8
1965	4.1	8.3

SOURCE: *Manpower Report of the President, 1966* (Washington, D.C.: Government Printing Office), p. 127.

Table 6.3 shows that unemployment rates for non-whites were generally over twice those of whites but that the rates varied with occupations for both racial categories. Table 6.4 shows considerable variation in white and non-white unemployment rates between the various age groups.

Although unemployment rates of nonwhites are about twice those of whites, and have increased markedly since 1953, between 1956 and 1963 nonwhite unemployment did not increase relative to total unemployment or as a proportion of total unemployment, as indicated by the data in Table 6.5. Actually, these statistics, which are selected for years which minimize the importance of the business cycle, show that nonwhite unemployment rates

TABLE 6.3

Unemployment Rates of Experienced Workers*
by Color and Major Occupation Group,
1955 and 1962

MAJOR OCCUPATION GROUP	WHITE		NONWHITE		NONWHITE AS PERCENTAGE OF WHITE	
	1962	1955	1962	1955	1962	1955
All occupation groups†	4.9%	3.5%	11.0%	7.7%	224%	208%
Clerical and sales workers	3.8	3.2	7.7	7.0	203	219
Craftsmen and foremen	4.8	3.9	9.7	8.8	202	226
Operatives	6.9	5.5	12.0	8.4	174	153
Private household workers	3.1	3.0	7.1	5.6	229	187
Other service workers	5.3	5.2	10.8	8.8	204	169
Laborers, except farm and mine	3.9	3.0	5.8	6.3	149	210
Farm laborers and foremen	11.0	9.8	15.8	12.1	144	123

* The base for the unemployment rate includes the employed, classified according to their current jobs, and the unemployed, classified according to their latest civilian job, if any; and excludes the unemployed persons who never held a full-time civilian job.

† Includes the following groups not shown separately: professional and technical workers; managers, officials, and proprietors; and farmers and farm managers.

SOURCE: Mathew A. Kessler, "Economic Status of Nonwhite Workers, 1955–62," Department of Labor, *Monthly Labor Review* (July 1963).

TABLE 6.4

Unemployment Rates, by Color, Age, and Sex, 1962

	UNEMPLOYMENT RATES			
	MALES		FEMALES	
AGE	White	Nonwhite	White	Nonwhite
14 years and over	4.6%	11.9%	5.5%	11.1%
14–19 years	12.3	20.7	11.5	28.2
20–24 years	8.0	14.6	7.7	18.2
25–34 years	3.8	10.5	5.4	11.5
35–44 years	3.1	8.6	4.5	8.9
45–54 years	3.5	8.3	3.7	7.1
55 years and over	4.1	10.1	3.5	3.6

SOURCE: Mathew A. Kessler, "Economic Status of Nonwhite Workers, 1955–1962," Department of Labor, *Monthly Labor Review* (July 1963), 3.

improved slightly relative to the totals between 1956 and 1963, suggesting that the *increases* in Negro unemployment rates are more cyclical than structural. This does not mean, of course, that the higher rates in 1956 and 1963 were not due to structural factors, or that significant structural changes did not occur before 1956.

TABLE 6.5

	Ratio of Unemployment in Each Group to National Unemployment Rate		Percentage of Total National Unemployment in Each Group	
	WHITE	NONWHITE	WHITE	NONWHITE
1956	.87	1.98	78.5%	21.5%
1959	.88	1.95	78.8	21.2
1962	.87	1.97	78.1	21.9
1963	.89	1.91	78.8	21.2

SOURCE: Adapted from R. A. Gordon, "Has Structural Unemployment Worsened?" *Industrial Relations* (May 1964), 71.

NEGRO EMPLOYMENT AND ECONOMIC GROWTH

In recent years, Negro unemployment rates seem to have changed at about twice the rate of total unemployment, whether the latter has been rising or falling. With respect to longer trends, a recent study of Negro and white employment patterns found no relationship between changes in Negro female and total employment, but concluded:

> In expanding fields Negro male employment has tended to grow at a faster rate than white male or total employment. . . . Even in slowly growing fields the employment of Negro men has nevertheless tended to increase at a faster rate than total employment or that of white men. . . . In rapidly declining fields, however, employment of Negro men has tended to decline more rapidly than that of white men both nationally and in the South.[5]

This suggests that Negroes would gain relatively from sustained growth as well as full employment. As the general unemployment rate is reduced, the nonwhite rate will decline, and if a rate of below 4 percent could be sustained while the rate of economic growth is increased and measures are taken to upgrade nonwhites, the income and employment gap between whites and nonwhites could be narrowed still further. The trends suggest, however, that extraordinary efforts will be required to bring Negro unemployment rates into line with those of whites. The 1966 *Report of the National Commission on Technology, Automation and the American Economy* concluded:

> If nonwhites continue to hold the same proportion of jobs in each occupation as in 1964, the nonwhite unemployment rate in 1975 will be more than five times that for the labor force as a whole. . . . If trends in the upgrading of nonwhites continue at the same rate as in recent years, the nonwhite unemployment rate in 1975 will be about 2½ times that for the labor force as a whole.

Factors Responsible for Racial Employment Patterns

The factors responsible for these Negro employment patterns are complex and interrelated, making it very difficult to determine the contribution to the total pattern made by each of them. It is, however, possible to discern the main factors responsible for these patterns. These are the heritages of the past, and the Negro's self-image and lack of education and training.

The most important impediment to the Negro's ability to improve his occupational position undoubtedly derives from the disadvantages he has suffered because of slavery, segregation, and discrimination. Not having worked in a variety of skilled, technical operations, Negroes have become stereotyped for certain jobs by employers, white workers, and even by themselves. Since the Negro has been regarded as inferior by many whites, those who would perpetuate a feeling of superiority for their crafts or occupations have tried to exclude Negroes.

Negroes also are restricted in their employment opportunities by a host of cultural and social factors. Since Negroes usually live in segregated neighborhoods, they rarely learn about jobs with few or no Negroes in them, and they apply for the kinds of jobs they know they can get. Since aspirations are conditioned by one's associates, few Negroes are motivated to apply for jobs from which they have been excluded.

EDUCATION

Negroes also are inadequately prepared through education and training to compete on an equal basis with whites. While the educational level of nonwhites is improving, the median is still below that of whites. Since education is related to income, the Negro's position is in some sense self-perpetuating. The median incomes of heads of families and their educational attainments in 1961 are shown in Table 6.6. These data indicate that

TABLE 6.6

EDUCATION	WHITE	NONWHITE	NONWHITE AS A PERCENTAGE OF WHITE
Elementary	$4,378	$2,539	58.0%
Less than 8 years	3,656	2,294	62.7
8 years	4,911	3,338	68.0
High school	6,186	3,863	64.2
1 to 3 years	5,882	3,449	58.6
4 years	6,390	4,559	71.3
College	8,288	6,444	77.8
1 to 3 years	7,344	5,525	74.2
4 years or more	9,315	7,875	84.5

SOURCE: Bureau of the Census, *Current Population Reports,* "Income of Families and Persons in the United States: 1961," Series P–60, No. 39.

as a general rule the ratio of nonwhite to white income increases with the level of education.

The percentage educational distributions of whites and nonwhites for various years are seen in Table 6.7. Only 25 percent of whites but 46 percent of nonwhites in the 18–24 age bracket had not completed high school in 1962, but there was a significant decline in the proportion of nonwhites who had less than five years of education and a marked increase in the proportion attending high school. Median nonwhite education lagged 3.8 years behind whites in 1952, 2.6 years in 1962, and 1.8 years in 1965.

These statistics do not tell the whole story, however, because it is well known that Negro education has been inferior to that of whites in the South and, according to the 1964 *Manpower Report of the President,* "although Negro students in the North receive a better education generally than Negroes (and many whites) in the South, their education still tends to be inferior to that of the northern white students with whom they will later compete for jobs." [6]

Negroes also are disadvantaged because at the same

TABLE 6.7

EDUCATION	WHITE					NONWHITE				
	1952	1957	1959	1962	1965	1952	1957	1959	1962	1965
Elementary										
Less than 5 years	5.2%	4.3%	3.7%	3.3%	2.7%	26.7%	21.2%	17.9%	15.5%	11.8%
5 to 8 years	29.3	25.8	23.6	21.4	18.9	38.7	34.9	34.3	29.8	25.7
High school										
1 to 3 years	18.7	19.0	19.4	18.8	18.4	15.9	19.3	20.6	23.2	24.9
4 years	28.3	30.8	32.0	33.5	36.8	10.8	14.8	15.8	21.0	24.4
College										
1 to 3 years	8.8	9.0	9.7	11.3	11.0	3.7	3.9	4.5	5.7	6.1
4 years or more	8.5	9.7	10.2	11.8	12.2	2.6	3.4	3.9	4.8	7.0
Median years completed	11.4	12.1	12.1	12.2	12.3	7.6	8.4	8.7	9.6	10.5

SOURCE: *Manpower Report of the President* (Washington, D.C.: Government Printing Office), p. 189.

level of education they have much more difficulty being absorbed into the labor force. Of the white high school graduates who last attended school in 1959, for instance, only 5.3 percent remained out of work 2.5 years after graduation as compared with 14.5 percent of nonwhite high school graduates. Of the 1959 dropouts, 10.2 percent of the whites and 18 percent of the nonwhites were unemployed two years later.[7] Thus nonwhite high school graduates had more trouble being absorbed by the labor force than white dropouts.

The Negroes' inadequate vocational and apprenticeship training also tends to perpetuate their employment in traditional jobs. The pattern in the South has been to have segregated vocational schools where Negroes were trained only for traditional occupations. While there are some excellent Negro vocational training schools associated with Negro colleges, many Negroes are barred from these programs because they are not high school graduates and are not admitted to apprentice programs because of discrimination.

Apprenticeship training is important because vocational training alone has rarely given students sufficient practical and theoretical training to equip them to become well-rounded craftsmen. A survey of training by the United States Department of Labor in 1963 disclosed that 16.6 percent of the 1.4 million workers taking formal training were in apprenticeship programs. The Labor Department's survey thus suggests that there were over 232,000 workers taking apprenticeship training, which is a much larger number than previous estimates had indicated. The 1960 census, for example, reported only 85,682 apprentices, 3.1 percent of whom were nonwhites.[8] The Labor Department survey also found that 35.3 million (55 percent) people in the civilian labor force between the ages of 22 and 64 had taken some formal training and in this group, apprenticeship training accounted for 8.2 percent. The most reliable estimate of the number of apprentices is the number in programs registered with the Bureau of Apprenticeship and Training. These figures indicate that there were about 160,000 in 1965, as compared with 230,000 in the peak 1950 year. Approximately 23,000 apprentices were graduated in 1963. Although apprenticeship training is not very important for many occupations, it accounted for the following proportions of the trades indicated in 1963.

TRADE	TOTAL TAKING FORMAL TRAINING (THOUSANDS)	PERCENTAGE TAKING APPRENTICE-SHIP TRAINING
Compositors and typesetters	171	30.6%
Construction craftsmen	2,708	43.9
Linemen and servicemen, telegraph, telephone, and power	260	36.8
Machinists	732	34.9
Meat cutters	132	56.1

SOURCE: *Manpower Report of the President, 1964*, Table F–9 (Washington, D.C.: Government Printing Office), p. 256.

Although statistics are not available on the proportion of nonwhites in the Labor Department's training survey, it is doubtful that more than 3 or 4 percent of these apprentices were Negroes. Therefore, although apprenticeship training could be an important means of getting Negroes into some occupations, unless there is a great expansion in the number of apprentices, not many Negroes will be able to improve their conditions through this means.

The Manpower Development and Training (MDTA), Area Redevelopment (ARA), and poverty (Economic Opportunity, EOA) programs offered some hope for improving the lot of minority groups. Although not as many nonwhites as whites were being trained for the higher-paying jobs in 1963, Tables 6.8 and 6.9 reveal that nonwhite representation was higher in the MDTA clerical, sales, skilled, and semi-skilled categories than the nonwhite employment distribution.

TABLE 6.8

MDTA Trainees and Total Nonwhite Employment by Occupation

OCCUPATIONAL GROUP	PERCENTAGE OF MDTA TRAINEES*		PERCENTAGE OF NONWHITE EMPLOYMENT (1962)
	TOTAL	NONWHITE	(1962)
	100.0%	100.0%	100.0%
Professional, managerial	8.6	7.9	7.9
Clerical, sales	23.0	19.0	8.8
Skilled	30.8	26.9	6.0
Semiskilled	25.4	29.6	19.9
Service	10.2	14.2	32.8
Other	2.0	2.3	24.6

* June 1963.

SOURCE: Statement by Seymour Wolfbein, Deputy Manpower Administrator, Department of Labor, before Senate Subcommittee on Manpower and Employment, June 6, 1963.

TABLE 6.9

Occupational Groups in Which MDTA Institutional Trainees Were Placed, 1965

OCCUPATIONAL GROUP	TOTAL	NONWHITE
Total	100.0%	100.0%
Service	15.0	22.0
Skilled	29.0	23.1
Semiskilled	18.9	19.8
Agricultural, unskilled	3.9	2.8
Professional, managerial	10.0	6.2
Clerical, sales	23.2	26.1

SOURCE: *1966 Report of the Secretary of Labor on Manpower Research and Training Under the MDTA* (Washington, D.C.: Government Printing Office), p. 21.

As Table 6.10 shows, the proportion of nonwhites increased from 30.4 percent of the trainees in MDTA projects in 1964 to 33.6 percent in 1965. Nonwhites also participate to a greater degree in MDTA programs than their proportion of the unemployed (20.3 percent). Non-

TABLE 6.10

Color and Sex of Enrollees in MDTA Institutional Projects, 1964 and 1965

COLOR AND SEX	PERCENTAGE DISTRIBUTION		
	MDTA ENROLLEES		ALL UNEMPLOYED PERSONS
	1965	1964	1965
Total Enrollees	100.0%	100.0%	100.0%
White	66.4	69.6	79.7
Nonwhite	33.6	30.4	20.3
White	100.0	100.0	100.0
Male	64.5	63.3	58.2
Female	35.6	36.7	41.8
Nonwhite	100.0	100.0	100.0
Male	51.8	53.6	53.7
Female	48.2	46.4	46.3

SOURCE: *1966 Report of the Secretary of Labor on Manpower Research and Training Under the MDTA* (Washington, D.C.: Government Printing Office), p. 12.

whites also constituted a high proportion of multioccupational projects (44.4 percent) and of those institutional enrollees declining basic education (51.9 percent).

Nevertheless, the MDTA and ARA programs have certain limitations from the standpoint of improving Negro employment opportunities. The programs are administered in cooperation with the states, and the requirement that programs be integrated has restricted the participation of several Southern states with large Negro concentrations. In 1961, for instance, the most ambitious single ARA plan undertaken during its first two years, a program to train some 1,200 equipment operators in the Yazoo Delta of Mississippi, where over 50 percent of the males were unemployed, had to be canceled because of the integration clause. And Louisiana refused to cooperate during the first two years of the program.[9]

In addition, very few Negroes have actually been trained under these programs. About 171,400 persons completed institutional training between August 1962 and December 1965.[10] If we assume nonwhites to be about 30 percent of this number, 51,420 nonwhites would have completed institutional training.

Although the MDTA programs were doing something to upgrade the Negro workforce, the figures in Table 6.8 indicate that nonwhites were not being upgraded relative to whites. Moreover, neither whites nor nonwhites were being trained at sufficient rates for professional and managerial jobs; indeed, the actual proportion of "professional" trainees probably was lower than indicated in Table 6.8 because the category used there includes "kindred workers" which inflates the total. The low participation of nonwhites in on-the-job training (OJT) programs is particularly disappointing because these jobs have significant advantages over institutional training. OJT is probably more meaningful than many of the institutional programs; and training on the job is more efficient because there is no placement problem, workers probably have greater motivation to learn, and they probably are trained on more modern equipment. Nonwhites constituted about 20 percent of all on-the-job trainees in 1964 and 1965. Since about 30,000 trainees completed OJT between August 1962 and the end of 1965, only about 6,000 nonwhites had benefited from this training.

If we assume nonwhites to have had the same placement experience as whites, about 43,700 nonwhites would have received jobs through MDTA training by the end of 1965. But the evidence suggests that Negro placement rates are lower than the white rates. Table 6.11 shows

TABLE 6.11

Employment Rate of White and Nonwhite Enrollees Who
Completed MDTA Institutional Training, 1965

OCCUPATIONAL GROUP	PERCENTAGE EMPLOYED	
	WHITE	NONWHITE
Semiprofessional, Technical	84.0%	89.7%
Licensed practical nurse	88.7	92.6
Draftsman	87.6	85.7
Clerical and Sales	65.8	53.6
General office clerk	65.4	50.3
Stenographer	61.8	51.6
Clerk-typist and typist	61.3	54.0
Service	69.4	65.0
Nurse aide, orderly, ward attendant	73.5	54.7
Skilled	80.8	66.1
Welder	79.6	71.7
Auto mechanic	81.8	56.4
Auto-body repairman	83.3	66.2
Semiskilled	74.4	61.7
General machine operator	84.6	73.9
Electronics assembler	70.6	70.9

SOURCE: *1966 Report of the Secretary of Labor on Manpower Research and Training Under the MDTA* (Washington, D.C.: Government Printing Office), p. 21.

that nonwhites generally had lower employment rates than whites except for the licensed practical nurse category. In a hospital training program in San Francisco, for example, 89 percent of whites but only 63 percent of nonwhites who completed the course were able to find jobs. Similar results were found in a study of the Armour and Company retraining program undertaken in connection with the closing of that company's Fort Worth plant in 1962. Although retrainees had much lower unemployment experiences than nonretrainees, of the Negro men who finished retraining by November 1963, 60 percent were in jobs unrelated to their training, as compared with only

20 percent for white male retrainees.[11] The Labor Department's 1963 training survey also found that the following proportions had never used their formal job training:

	Males	Females
Nonwhites	34%	26%
All Workers	20	16

Only 43 percent of nonwhites, but 60 percent of all workers, were using their training on their current jobs.[12]

MANAGEMENT ATTITUDES

Management has major responsibility for the hiring and upgrading of Negroes in on-the-job training programs, whether these are sponsored by MDTA or not. And for many reasons, relatively few Negroes participate in OJT programs. For one thing, since it frequently has been assumed that Negroes will not be promoted to skilled or managerial positions, management has hired Negroes who are generally unqualified for promotion.

There is, moreover, ample evidence that management is prejudiced against using Negroes in skilled and supervisory categories. Although there have been some important recent changes in management's thinking, the traditional attitudes seem to be that Negroes are not suited for skilled jobs or that customers or white workers will react unfavorably to job integration. One management official, sympathetic to the upgrading of Negroes, described a common management view of the use of Negroes in skilled positions:

> Negroes, basically and as a group, with only rare exceptions, are not as well trained for higher skills and jobs as whites. They appear to be excellent for work, usually unskilled, that requires stamina and brawn—and little else. They are unreliable and cannot adjust to the demands of a factory.[13]

A Connecticut study found that management explained the absence of Negroes from skilled positions this way:

Negroes are not "by nature" suited for skilled work and are better suited for heavy, unskilled jobs; Negroes do not apply for skilled jobs; Negroes do not possess the skills to do the skilled jobs; they lack education.[14]

A San Francisco study found that employers refused to hire and upgrade Negroes for the following reasons: fear of customer or employee reaction; tradition; and the belief that Negroes are bad credit risks and get involved in heavy debts. About one-third of the San Francisco employers mentioned physical, mental, or social traits that disqualified Negroes for certain jobs, as illustrated by the following statements concerning Negroes: "not orderly—do not have an organized mind," "not intelligent enough to hold higher jobs," "not put in executive training positions because we don't expect them to be and they don't expect to get to be top management," "could not pass the physical examination, especially with regard to venereal disease." "They are not interested in working up because of the grief and responsibility involved. They don't want responsibility." This study concluded that employers who had hired Negroes seem less prejudiced than those who had not but that there "appeared to be a consensus among some employers that nonwhites lacked motivation for advancement to higher supervisory positions." [15]

A Birmingham study found that management attributed limited opportunity for Negroes to the following factors: education and training; the inability to use Negroes where they must meet the public; fear of the reaction of white workers (it was found, however, that where whites dominated the workforce before unionization, there tended to be more friction after unions came in); belief that Negroes lack a sense of responsibility; separate rest rooms would have to be installed; Negro workers are "well suited" to the type of work they are performing and are more productive than whites in jobs requiring a lot of strength, or which are repetitive or require intense heat.[16]

Noland and Bakke found that Negroes were not hired for skilled jobs because of management's belief that Negroes were not acceptable to white workers, had insufficient training, were careless in work habits, and were not self-reliant.[17] They also found that some managements believed that Negroes were "not as capable as whites for production jobs. Their intelligence is believed to be lower and their training less varied and adequate . . . are slow learners . . . unreliable, irresponsible, lazy, overbearing, sensitive, unambitious, restless, and unpersevering." [18]

These results were also found in a study by the Urban League in New Orleans and by the New York State Commission Against Discrimination.[19] Management has historically preferred Negro workers for certain kinds of jobs or for certain of their presumed attributes. Since there is a tendency for whites to leave undesirable jobs when economic conditions improve, management has found that Negroes are more dependable in these occupations because they are "locked in" by limited alternatives. Moreover, many managers believe that Negroes are "better suited" than whites for hot, disagreeable work requiring great physical strength. Employers also have historically been willing to hire Negroes because of racial wage differentials and because Negroes were considered to be safeguards against unionism. The great transformations wrought by the New Deal, the CIO, and World War II almost eliminated this factor, however, because they virtually abolished racial wage differentials in the same job classification and changed the Negro community's antiunion attitudes.

Of course, management prejudices have been counter-acted by other developments. One is changes in general labor market conditions. Thus, Negroes made great occupational gains during the labor shortages accompanying World Wars I and II. The general pattern seems to have been that when white males were not available, white women would be hired if they could do the work and were available, then Negro men and women would be hired in that order. In the South Carolina textile industry, for example, employment of white males declined from 62 percent of the total to 51.8 percent between 1940 and 1945, while the employment of white females increased their proportion from 34 percent to 43.1 percent and Negro males from 3.9 percent to 5.1 percent. In all manufacturing in South Carolina, which tends to be dominated by low wage employment, white males declined 9.7 percent during these years and white females increased by 8.2 percent while Negro males increased .2 percent and Negro females by 1.3 percent.[20]

The supply of labor is a very important consideration because management would be more willing to hire Negroes if there were enough Negro craftsmen to do the work if the whites quit (which they will rarely do in good industrial jobs) or boycott particular employers (which is relatively easy to do in construction work). Moreover, the knowledge that there are enough Negroes to do the work will usually deter whites who might otherwise be inclined to quit when Negroes are hired. But where jobs are less desirable, the introduction of Negroes sometimes has caused whites to quit and be replaced by Negroes. Thus, if the employer has had some other reason to hire or promote Negroes, like wartime labor shortages or pressure from the Negro community or governmental agencies, he has been inclined to do so if the supply of Negroes is adequate.

THE INFLUENCE OF UNIONS

Employers are directly responsible for the racial employment patterns in most manufacturing jobs, but unions have been more responsible for racial employment patterns on the railroads and in the construction and printing trades, since unions are often strong enough in these occupations to control the supply of labor and maintain *de facto* closed shop conditions; they have thus been able to deny Negroes employment in the skilled trades by barring them from union membership. While they are not primarily responsible for industrial racial employment patterns, unions have perpetuated those patterns by maintaining segregated seniority rosters. Moreover, job segregation was often formalized by having different unions in each craft, as is true, for instance, among longshoremen and on the railroads.

Negroes have greater employment opportunities in the nonunion sectors of some building trades crafts, such as electricians and plumbers, but there is no evidence that nonunion manufacturing establishments have hired or upgraded more Negroes. Indeed, the virtually unorganized Southern textile industry has had very few Negro employees and yet has maintained rigid racial segregation. Almost without exception, moreover, those firms which have desegregated their lines of progression in the South are unionized. The union can be accused of discrimination, however, where it fails to apply contracts equally and permits "informal" discriminatory practices to continue in violation of the contract.

Even though most of its efforts in this direction have been more for trade union than for racial reasons, organized labor has done many positive things to improve Negro job opportunities. For one thing, unions have introduced the principle of seniority, which has made it possible for Negroes to hold their jobs when those jobs become more attractive to whites during recessions or when employers are induced to displace Negroes with whites because wages are equalized. The principle of seniority also has been used to make it possible for Negroes to advance occupationally within many unionized firms. This is not to argue, of course, that all labor organizations have done what they should to protect the Negro's seniority rights. But the fact that discrimination *tended* to weaken seniority was a factor *undermining* discrimination by unions.

At the national level, the labor movement has contributed decisively to fights for civil rights, improved education, and other social legislation. Unions also have used their collective bargaining power to negotiate nondiscrimination agreements, which existed in about one-fifth of all major collective bargaining contracts in 1961.[21] Especially important nondiscrimination agreements were reached between the United Auto Workers and the Ford,

General Motors, Chrysler, and American Motors companies in 1961 and between the Steelworkers and eleven major steel companies in 1964 (Armco, Bethlehem, Colorado Fuel and Iron, Great Lakes Steel, Inland, Jones and Laughlin, Pittsburgh Steel, Republic, United States Steel, Wheeling, and Youngstown Sheet and Tube).

In addition, as will be seen in the following chapter, the mere presence of a union in the plant has given Negro workers rights they would not otherwise have had. Not only can Negroes sue for the abrogation of specific contract rights, but the union is required by the courts, and more recently by the National Labor Relations Board, to follow nondiscrimination policies with respect to all workers in the bargaining unit.

Finally, unions have promoted Negro interests as a part of the basic equalitarian rationale of trade unionism. Union leaders fully realize that their organizations are weakened if they fail to promote equal seniority, wage, and other benefits for all workers regardless of race. Fringe benefits and the elimination of occupational wage differentials also help Negroes, who have been concentrated in lower job categories.

Chapter VII

NEGRO EMPLOYMENT
AND PUBLIC POLICY

The movement of Negroes from rural to urban areas has increased their political power and has naturally led to demands that government at all levels do something to eradicate discrimination in employment as well as in education, voting, public accommodations, and housing. Indeed, without better employment opportunities, many of these other rights are of little value. As a consequence, Negroes have demanded equal rights to government jobs and to those supported by Federal funds, and a number of government agencies have been established to implement public policies against discrimination. The most important expressions of public policy against discrimination in employment have been the Committee on Fair Employment Practices (FEPC) created by President Franklin D. Roosevelt in 1941, the various government contract committees appointed by every President since the New Deal, the FEP

laws passed in twenty-five states and a number of municipalities, court rulings and NLRB decisions which require
unions to represent Negroes fairly, and the Civil Rights
Act of 1964.

President Roosevelt's Committees on
Fair Employment Practice

President Roosevelt issued the executive order creating
the first FEPC in August 1941, after A. Philip Randolph
organized a movement to lead fifty thousand Negroes in
a march on Washington to protest discrimination in employment. This executive order gave the committee power
to "receive and investigate complaints of discrimination"
in defense industries and allied work and to "take appropriate steps to redress the grievances it finds to be
valid." But, in spite of this relatively wide jurisdiction
(much broader than that of the government contract
committees created by subsequent Presidents), the first
FEPC was no match for the combined power of its Southern
congressional critics and the railroad unions and employers,
and the committee's proposed railroad hearings met such
staunch opposition that in January 1943 they were in-
definitely postponed, an action that was followed by the
resignation of a number of key personnel who could not
be replaced because of the committee's obvious impotence.

However, the FEPC's supporters succeeded in getting
a new executive order in June 1943, creating another
committee with enlarged powers. The second committee
was placed in the Office of Emergency Management, given
additional financial support, allowed to create twelve
branch offices, and empowered to police an antidiscrimination clause to be included in government contracts. This
order stated that it was

> . . . the policy of the United States that there shall
> be no discrimination in the employment of any person
> in war industries or in Government by reason of race,
> creed, color or national origin, and . . . it is the duty
> of all employers, including the several Federal depart-
> ments and agencies, and all labor organizations . . . to

eliminate discrimination in regard to hire, tenure, terms or conditions of employment, or union membership.

Although civil rights groups tried to create a permanent FEPC when the war was over, their efforts were blocked by Southern congressmen, and the FEPC was crippled by the 1944 Russell Amendment, which prohibited the use of funds by the President to pay the expenses of any agency unless Congress appropriated funds for that purpose.[1]

Thus, the FEPC had very limited powers to deal with discrimination in employment. The main factor weakening the committee was congressional opposition, which not only gave moral support to its enemies, but also denied the organization sufficient economic and political power to carry out its functions. The committee had no power to compel compliance with its orders or, as is customary with administrative agencies created by Congress, to seek the aid of Federal courts in compelling such compliance. In a showdown, the committee had only such power as the President saw fit to give it in that particular case. The President was sometimes willing to give his moral support by personally intervening in a case, but in the face of widespread defiance, this technique could have only limited effectiveness because the President did not have time to intervene in many cases. Under attack by hostile critics, who questioned its legitimacy because it lacked congressional approval, the committee was forced to proceed slowly and cautiously.

The foregoing does not mean, however, that the FEPC had no effect on discrimination. The committee received only the most difficult cases which could not be settled by other agencies, and served as a safety valve through which pent-up resentments could be expressed. Furthermore, some employers and unions who wanted to increase job opportunities for Negroes used the committee as an excuse for their actions. The committee thus became the scapegoat for some unpopular, "messy" decisions. Finally, although the committee's hearings and orders often were indecisive in the short run, they added their weight to a long stream of moral indictments of racial discrimination that produced the state FEPC laws, court decisions against discrimination, and the government contract committees, to be discussed below.

The President's Committee on Government Contracts

The President's Committee on Government Contracts (PCGC) was created by President Eisenhower in 1953 to promote equal employment opportunities for all qualified workers either employed or seeking employment covered by government contracts. In order to achieve this objective, it became the responsibility of the head of each agency of the Federal Government to obtain compliance with the nondiscrimination clause in any contract or subcontract entered into or amended by that agency. The committee transmitted complaints to the contracting agencies and these agencies reported to the PCGC concerning the investigation of those complaints.

The precise acts prohibited by President Eisenhower's executive order included, but were not limited to, the following: employment, upgrading, demotion or transfer; recruitment or recruitment advertising; layoff or termination; rates of pay or other forms of compensation; and apprenticeship and other training programs.

The PCGC relied upon "education, conciliation, mediation and persuasion" to enforce the nondiscrimination clause, though in 1957 the committee's chairman, Vice-President Richard Nixon, instructed contracting agencies to take a "firmer approach" where these methods did not "bring about proper results." [2] The Vice-President requested that the agencies consider the past employment records of contractors in awarding contracts and "deny awards, as appropriate, upon determination by your agency of clear and convincing evidence of noncompliance by Government contractors with the standard nondiscrimination clause." [3] However, no contracts were ever canceled for this reason.

The forces limiting the PCGC's power were similar to

those which frustrated the FEPC. The lack of explicit congressional approval denied it sufficient funds and power. The Russell Amendment made it difficult for the committee to proceed directly against unions, caused heavy reliance on the (perhaps unsympathetic) contracting agencies for enforcement, and introduced an inefficient and complex enforcement structure. In the final analysis, of course, the general impression projected by the government determines the reaction of contractors to fair employment programs, and the prevailing opinion, which proved well founded, was that contracts would not be revoked by the PCGC for violations of the nondiscrimination clauses. And when complaints were filed with the committee, it seemed willing to settle for very limited corrections.

In spite of these limitations, however, the PCGC made a positive contribution to the cause of equal employment opportunities. In the South, where there were no state FEP laws, the committee's existence, its educational activities, and the frequent statements of Vice-President Nixon branded racial discrimination as immoral and contrary to public policy. Moreover, the importance of government contracts was such that civil rights groups were able to use the committee as a vehicle for publicizing discrimination and getting at least a change in formal racial policies—in the petroleum refining industry, the PCGC was one of the factors producing elimination of separate lines of progression. The PCGC also clarified some issues and pointed up certain weaknesses, developed considerable information on Negro employment problems, and formed the basis for the Committee on Equal Employment Opportunity.

The President's Committee on Equal Employment Opportunity

The President's Committee on Equal Employment Opportunity (PCEEO), appointed by President Kennedy in March 1961, assumed a much more aggressive posture than its predecessor. The PCEEO was given the responsibility for policing antidiscrimination programs within

Federal employment as well as with government contractors. The PCEEO program went beyond the mere agreement not to discriminate; it attempted to get Federal contractors to take affirmative action to eliminate discrimination and to see that recruitment, hiring, and upgrading programs were undertaken on a nondiscriminatory basis. The committee also required contractors to notify labor unions with which they dealt of their fair employment policies, to see that nondiscrimination clauses were included in their subcontracts, to file regular compliance reports with the committee, and to make records available for inspection.

Moreover, the PCEEO was empowered to publish the names of noncomplying contractors and unions, recommend legal action by the Justice Department to prosecute those who failed to comply or furnished false information, cancel the contracts of noncomplying contractors, and prohibit government agencies from entering into new contracts with discriminating employers who had not demonstrated changes in their policies.

A significant new approach by the PCEEO was the voluntary Plans for Progress program for employers and the Programs for Fair Practices for unions. These plans seek to eliminate discrimination through cooperation, and by February 1965, over three hundred companies with more than 8,250,000 employees had signed plans for progress. Under the union plans, signed by one hundred eighteen internationals representing over 90 percent of the AFL-CIO's membership, labor organizations agreed to: accept all qualified members on a nondiscriminatory basis; work to ensure equal job opportunities for all workers; abolish segregated local unions; and work with management to get antidiscrimination clauses in collective agreements, eliminate discrimination in apprenticeship programs, and abolish segregated facilities in plants.

The scope of the order creating the PCEEO was extended in June 1963 to cover all federally assisted construction contracts and in February 1964 to include discrimination because of age where age was not a bona fide occupational qualification. In 1963 the Secretary of Labor announced objective standards to be used in the selection of apprentices registered with the Bureau of Apprenticeship and Training (BAT), but opposition from the construction industry delayed the adoption of these standards until January 1964. The building trades unions vigorously opposed government intervention in their industry, especially what they considered to be the Labor Department's efforts to get preferential treatment for Negroes, but in spite of this opposition the original standards remained virtually unchanged. The new rules permitted selection of apprentices on the basis of (1) qualifications based on objective standards, (2) demonstration of equality of opportunity, or (3) assurance of equality of opportunity to the satisfaction of the BAT. Equality can be shown by the racial composition of the workforce, though the rules disclaim any intention of establishing specific quotas.

Apprenticeship programs that did not meet these standards could be deregistered, which meant that employers in these programs could not have paid apprentice wages on Federal projects, and might have lost draft deferment for apprentices. These were obviously weak penalties where employers and unions were recalcitrant, as in some building trades. Indeed, one of the reasons for the Labor Department's long delay in implementing the rules was the realization that in the absence of stronger penalties, the decertification of an apprenticeship program was not a very effective remedy. It was also because of this that in February 1965 the PCEEO told the General Services Administration not to award contracts to a group of contractors without first obtaining permission from the committee, an action that was taken because the "cited contractors were not able to obtain workers from nondiscriminatory sources." [4] Discrimination in apprenticeship training also was made an illegal employment practice by the Civil Rights Act of 1964. Thus, although the Federal registration program was a very weak weapon against discrimination in apprenticeship training, it was followed by a wide range of Federal and state penalties against this form of discrimination.

While the PCEEO took a more direct approach to unions than did the PCGC, its penalties affected unions through the employer, which, some observers feel, reduced its effectiveness. The committee has been attacked by the NAACP's labor secretary for having provided only "symbolic breakthroughs" on the technical and professional level, but "very little real change for the Negro industrial worker." [5] Moreover, the United States Commission on Civil Rights (USCCR) noted in 1961 that while the PCEEO had "taken steps to overcome obstacles encountered by [the PCGC]" much more was required, including a re-affirmation that "when Government contractors completely delegate to labor organizations the power of hiring, or of determining admission to apprenticeship training programs or other terms and conditions of employment, they will be held responsible for discriminatory acts of the unions." In a report two years later, the USCCR noted some progress along these lines,[6] particularly the Programs for Fair Progress. While these pledges are "relatively meaningless in terms of legal obligation since the signatory internationals have no power to compel compliance by their member locals, [they] do commit the AFL-CIO and the internationals to full cooperation" with the PCEEO.[7] The denial of Federal contracts where the Department of Labor decides that discrimination exists in apprenticeship programs is a potent threat.

Finally, the PCEEO's Plans for Progress (PFP) have caused some controversy among civil rights experts. The plans are criticized for relying on "voluntarism," which has not proved effective. Proponents, on the other hand, point out that the plans apply to unions and firms not covered by government contracts, making it possible for the PCEEO to expand its scope. Moreover, the statistics confirm that PFP companies have expanded their employment of Negroes. These plans originated in May 1961, and of ninety-one companies reported on as of July 1963, total employment had increased by 12.4 percent and non-white employment 14.7 percent, or by 27,180 employees. Employment of salaried workers increased by 13.8 percent, but nonwhite employment in these categories increased by 23.5 percent. Of these nonwhite salaried employees, 3,266 were placed in management, professional, sales, and technical jobs, and 2,884 in clerical and office positions. The increase in nonwhite hourly employment was distributed as follows:[8]

Craftsmen	1,964
Operatives	17,557
Service	971
Laborers	538

Employment in PFP companies increased by 60,000 between September and November 1963, and 25 percent of the new employees were nonwhites. In comparable periods before the PFP program, nonwhite employment would have increased by about 3 percent.[9] These job increases are important, considering that much effort is required to produce additional jobs for nonwhites. For example, after all the demonstrations in New York during the summer of 1963, by December 1963, only about 111 Negroes and Puerto Ricans gained entry into unions as journeymen or apprentices, and only 3,121 applications were received in spite of a vigorous campaign.[10] And in spite of much agitation after 1953 to eliminate job segregation in the Southern petroleum refining industry, a study of eleven companies revealed that by 1960 only about 550 Negroes had been promoted. Of that number, 364 promotions were in two companies and 24 were temporary appointments.[11]

It should not be concluded, however, that the voluntary programs by themselves would have produced these results. It is significant that the "voluntary" plans came at a time of increasing militancy by civil rights groups. Equally significant, all but one of the thirty-five largest government defense contractors in 1962 were among the first ninety-one companies to sign plans for progress. Indeed, defense contracts accounted for over half of the total sales for seventeen of these thirty-five largest companies in 1962.[12]

In 1965, President Johnson abolished the PCEEO, and its contract compliance functions were transferred to the United States Department of Labor. The committee's government employee nondiscrimination functions were transferred to the Civil Service Commission, and the PFP program was continued as a separate program on a voluntary, private basis. These changes were made at the suggestion of Vice-President Humphrey "to streamline and strengthen" the antidiscrimination programs.

State Fair Employment Practice Laws

Since World War II, enforceable fair employment practice (FEP) laws have been passed in twenty-five states and many municipalities.[13] By 1964, these laws covered virtually the entire nonwhite population outside the South and prohibited discrimination by employers and employment agencies as well as unions. The laws are usually administered by commissioners, who are part-time officials in every state except New York. The powers relating to the adjustment of complaints are fairly uniform and include: (1) the power to receive, investigate and pass upon complaints alleging discrimination in employment; (2) where investigation reveals probable cause for crediting the allegations, the duty to eliminate these practices by conference, conciliation, and persuasion; (3) the power to conduct public hearings, subpoena witnesses and compel their attendance, administer oaths, take testimony of any person under oath, and to require the production of any books or papers relating to matters before the commissions; (4) the power to seek court orders enforcing subpoenas and cease and desist orders; and (5) the power to undertake studies of discrimination and publish the results.

Since so many other factors were at work influencing racial employment patterns besides the state FEP laws, it is difficult to determine their impact. A careful study of these laws concludes, however, that they have definitely improved the employment opportunities of minorities, particularly in such states as New York and New Jersey and in Philadelphia, which have relatively well-financed and well-staffed enforcement agencies.[14] These commissions have caused many companies, unions, and employment agencies to alter their discriminatory practices and have opened the door to employment in thousands of cases. Union referral systems have been regularized and a number of the most recalcitrant craft unions in the construction and railroad industries have been forced to admit Negroes or abolish discriminatory provisions in their constitutions. Indeed, as noted in Chapter III, one of the main factors causing unions to remove the formal racial restrictions in their constitutions was the passage of the New York, New Jersey, and Connecticut FEP laws.

In spite of these accomplishments, however, civil rights groups have been very critical of the effects of state FEP laws. It is significant that the racial demonstrations in Northern cities during 1963 and 1964 were in states and municipalities with the most active FEP commissions. Negroes are dissatisfied with the rate of change in racial employment patterns, partly because they probably expected too much from the commissions, whose case-by-case approach is bound to produce results only slowly. Moreover, it is not always easy to prove discrimination where it is thought to exist. Large percentages of the cases are found to be without merit. Sometimes the practices complained of are very complicated and operate to restrict employment to a particular group. Moreover, during times of growing unemployment, racial employment patterns will change very slowly because of limited changes in total employment.

The Courts

Negroes have also used the courts to overcome discrimination by unions and employers, although most court cases have dealt with unions because employers have had no legal obligation to follow nondiscrimination policies in the absence of legislation or contract provisions to the contrary. The same is not true of unions, however, because they acquire legal rights and duties as a result of the National Labor Relations and Railway Labor Acts. The United States Supreme Court has ruled, therefore, that the Constitution imposes upon unions which acquire the privilege of exclusive bargaining rights under these acts the duty to represent all members of the bargaining unit fairly.[15] Some Federal courts also have held that employers are jointly liable with unions for maintaining fair representation,[16] and aggrieved minorities have brought suit against unions for damages resulting from violation of their legal rights. Although court action requires a great deal of time, has an uncertain outcome, and has rarely resulted in damages to the plaintiffs, lawsuits are valuable to aggrieved minorities as a threat to discriminating employers and unions, and injunctions have been used to make it possible for Negroes to retain their jobs.[17]

The National Labor Relations Board

The National Labor Relations Board (NLRB) traditionally has been much more cautious than the courts in interpreting and applying its power to prevent discrimination. Before 1964, the board had declared that "neither exclusion from membership nor segregated membership per se represents evasion on the part of a labor organization of its statutory duty of 'equal representation.' " [18] This caution undoubtedly was dictated by Congress's repeated refusal to give the board specific authority to deal with racial discrimination.

In a number of recent cases, however, especially the 1964 Hughes Tool decision, the board has made an important departure, which, if sustained by the Federal courts, could have important consequences for discrimination in employment.[19] Specifically reversing previous NLRB decisions, the board ruled, in a split decision, in Hughes Tool that *a violation of the duty of fair representation is also an unfair labor practice*. Previously, the NLRB had interpreted its authority in such cases as limited to the relatively weak and rarely used penalty of revoking a union's certification. An exception was the 1962 Miranda case, which did not involve racial discrimination, and here the board had ruled that a violation of the duty of fair representation was an unfair labor practice.[20] But a United States Court of Appeals created some uncertainty about this doctrine by refusing to enforce the NLRB's Miranda decision.[21] Although the board's interpretation in this case is of doubtful validity in view of the Miranda case and Congress's past refusal to give it the power which it has assumed, if the Supreme Court agrees that the union's violation of its duty of fair representation is also an unfair labor practice, the board can issue cease and desist orders enforceable in the Federal courts. The Hughes Tool theory would in effect give the aggrieved person an administrative remedy for the duty of fair representation, making it no longer necessary for him to seek relief in the courts. Relying on the Hughes Tool doctrine, the board ruled in 1964 that a Rubber Workers' local in Gadsden, Alabama, had committed an unfair labor practice by refusing to process grievances against job discrimination and segregated plant facilities.[22]

The Civil Rights Act of 1964

Title VII of the Civil Rights Act of 1964, which became effective in July 1965, bans discrimination in employment because of race, color, religion, national origin, or sex. Title VII applies to all employers who are engaged in an industry affecting commerce and who have 25 or more employees for each working day in each of twenty or more calendar weeks in the current or preceding calendar year, but this does not include the government of the United States, an Indian tribe, a state or political subdivision of a state, or a private membership club (other than labor unions). The act applies only to persons having fewer than 100 employees the first year, 75 employees the second year, 50 employees the third year, and 25 employees thereafter. Similar qualifications apply to unions with the corresponding number of members until the third year, when it applies to unions with 25 members. Although the government of the United States is exempt, the law stipulates that it shall be the policy of the United States government to insure equal employment opportunities for Federal employees and that the President shall use his power to effectuate this policy.

ADMINISTRATION

The Civil Rights Act creates an Equal Employment Opportunity Commission (EEOC) of five members (no more than two from either major political party), appointed by the President with the advice and consent of the Senate. The EEOC has power to receive complaints of racial discrimination, to attempt to settle these complaints through informal "conference, conciliation, and persuasion," and, if such measures fail, a civil action may be brought in Federal district court by the aggrieved party. The district court may also issue an injunction against the discriminating party. The United States Attorney General is empowered to bring civil action whenever "he has reasonable cause to believe that any person or group of persons is engaged in a practice of resistance to the full enjoyment of any of the rights secured" by Title VII. If the Attorney General certifies that a case brought by an aggrieved individual is in the public interest, the court may permit him to intervene in the private civil suit. If the court's order in the civil action is not obeyed, the EEOC is authorized to "commence proceedings to compel compliance with such orders."

The Civil Rights Act does not supersede the state FEP laws unless those laws specifically permit or require an act made unlawful by the Civil Rights Act. Indeed, the Federal law specifically prohibits the filing of a complaint with the EEOC, until

> . . . sixty days after proceedings have been commenced under the State or local law, unless such proceedings have been earlier terminated, provided that such sixty-day period shall be extended to one hundred and twenty days during the first year after the effective date of such State or local law.

If a charge is filed with the commission concerning an unlawful practice occurring in a state or local area with an antidiscrimination law, the EEOC is required to "notify the appropriate State or local officials and, upon request, afford them a reasonable time . . . to act under such State or local law to remedy the practice alleged." The EEOC announced in December 1965 that unions and employers would be notified of complaints against them after the complainants had been interviewed. This procedure is in line with the EEOC's policy of attempting to settle cases by conciliation and other informal means.

PROHIBITED ACTS

Section 703(a) of Title VII makes it an unlawful employment practice for an employer to discriminate in any way against any individual "with respect to his compensation, terms, conditions, or privileges of employment" because of race, color, religion, sex, or national origin. Discrimination in hiring, discharge, or conditions of employment are prohibited by this section, which also explicitly prohibits segregation or classification of employees on the basis of the five forbidden criteria.

It is an unlawful employment practice, according to Section 703(b), for an employment agency either to "refer or to fail or refuse to refer for employment, or otherwise to discriminate against, any individual" on the basis of race, color, religion, sex, or national origin.

Section 703(c) makes it an unlawful employment practice for a labor organization:

1. to exclude or to expel from its membership, or otherwise to discriminate against, any individual. . . .
2. to limit, segregate, or classify its membership, or to classify or fail or refuse to refer for employment any individual, in any way which would deprive . . . [him] of employment opportunities, or would limit such employment opportunities or otherwise adversely affect his status as an employee or as an applicant for employment. . . .
3. to cause or attempt to cause an employer to discriminate against an individual in violation of this section.

Section 703(c) thus clearly prohibits exclusion from membership, segregated locals, and discrimination in referrals. Section 703(d) makes it an unlawful employment practice for any employer, labor organization, or joint labor-management committee controlling apprenticeship or other training to discriminate in training programs on the basis of the five forbidden criteria.

Section 704(b) makes it an unlawful employment practice for an employer, labor organization, or employment agency to publish or cause to be published any advertisement or notice indicating a preference, limitation, specification, or discrimination on the basis of the five forbidden criteria, except "when religion, sex, or national origin is a bona fide occupational qualification for employment."

QUALIFICATIONS

Although race and color are never considered to be bona fide occupational qualifications, Section 703(e) provides that it shall not be an unlawful employment practice for employers, labor organizations, labor-management apprenticeship and training committees, or employment agencies to discriminate on the basis of religion, sex, or national origin where these three criteria are "reasonably necessary to the normal operation of that particular business or enterprise. . . ." Section 703(e) also provides that it shall *not* be an unlawful employment practice for religious schools, colleges, universities, or other educational institutions to hire employees on the basis of a particular religion if such institution is "in whole or in substantial part, owned, supported, controlled, or managed" by a particular religion or if the curriculum of such institution "is directed toward the propagation of a particular religion."

Sections 703(f) through 703(j) add other exceptions to the prohibitions in Title VII. Section 703(f) provides that the phrase "unlawful employment practice" shall not extend to action taken against any person who is a member of the Communist party of the United States or who is a member of an organization required to register as a Communist-action or Communist-front organization by a final order to the Subversive Activities Control Board under the provisions of the Subversive Activities Control Act of 1950. However, this provision would appear to have very little practical effect because discrimination based on political beliefs is not unlawful.

Section 703(g) provides that it shall not be an unlawful employment practice to discriminate against persons who have not fulfilled or have ceased to fulfill national security requirements in any position "where the occupancy of such position, or access to the premises in or upon which any part of the duties of such position is performed or is to be performed," is subject to national security requirements imposed by United States statute or executive order of the President. This would again appear to be a qualification of very little practical importance because discrimination in such a case would be for lack of security clearance and not because of race.

Section 703(h) provides that it shall not be an unlawful employment practice for employers to apply different standards of compensation or different terms or conditions of employment where these are based on a bona fide seniority or merit system or where these different conditions are applied to workers in different locations and the "differences are not the result of an intention to discriminate" because of the five forbidden criteria. Here we have another unnecessary qualification because nothing in Title VII could be interpreted as preventing differentials based on bona fide seniority, merit, or geographical criteria where these are uniformly applied to all workers.

In what promises to be one of the most troublesome qualifications, Section 703(h) also provides that it shall not be an unlawful employment practice for an employer to pay wage differentials based on sex where these differentials are permitted by the 1963 equal pay amendment to the Fair Labor Standards Act. Section 703(i) makes it lawful for employers near Indian reservations to continue to give preference to Indians living on or near these reservations. Finally, Section 703(j) provides that nothing in

Title VII "shall be interpreted to require any employer, employment agency, labor organization, or joint labor-management committee subject to this title to grant preferential treatment to any individual or to any group." As we shall see later, the question of preferential treatment is not likely to be settled by this provision.

Since the foregoing list of acts prohibited by Title VII of the Civil Rights Act generally covers most of the main forms of discrimination in employment, the major controversies of the future are likely to concern matters of interpretation and enforcement rather than acts prohibited. However, some problems are likely to be caused by the difficulty of interpreting the meaning of the various acts prohibited. For example, section 706(g) provides that judicial relief is available only if the courts find that a respondent "intentionally engaged in, or is intentionally engaging in unlawful employment practices." Perhaps the distinction between "intentional" and "unintentional" discrimination will be clearer to the courts than at first seems likely. Surely, however, if discrimination were unintentional in the sense that it was incidental to the operation of a test, merit, or seniority system, adequate defense could be made without the confusion that is likely to exist in determining whether or not discrimination is intentional.

A question might also be raised concerning the provision which makes discrimination on the basis of national origin a bona fide occupational qualification. It is very difficult to conceive of cases where such a bona fide occupational qualification might exist. The example of a French or Italian cook is unconvincing because the bona fide qualification would appear to be the ability to prepare French or Italian cuisine. Similarly, language competency would appear to be the bona fide occupational qualification and not national origin.

Section 703(h) is an important exception because it has the effect of narrowing the coverage of Title VII. This section provides that it will not be an unlawful employment practice for an employer to "differentiate upon the basis of sex" in wage payments if such differentiation is authorized by the 1963 equal pay amendments to the Fair Labor Standards Act (FLSA). The main difference between Title VII and the FLSA is coverage, since the latter contains numerous specific exemptions and relates only to workers engaged in interstate commerce or in producing goods for commerce whereas the former relates to workers in industries "affecting commerce." Thus, those employers who are covered by the CRA and exempt from the FLSA apparently may sometimes legally discriminate in wage payments but not in hiring.

Title VII's prohibitions against discrimination because of sex also create possible conflicts between various state laws and the CRA. Presumably, for example, certain state limitations on the conditions under which women may be hired would create bona fide occupational disqualifications where the practice prohibited by the state law was important to a particular employer.

Of course, the most troublesome area created by the prohibitions against discrimination based on sex undoubtedly will involve the common practice of giving different privileges and benefits to female workers. It would presumably be possible for male employees to demand equal conditions in these cases.

The Problem of Preferential Treatment

Demands by civil rights groups for preferential treatment for minorities are based upon the realization that even with nondiscriminatory employment policies, Negroes would not be able to change their employment patterns very rapidly. Although preferential treatment is usually condemned by employers, union leaders, and most government agencies, it has been surprisingly common. It works like this: when Negroes have brought pressures for access to jobs from which they have been barred, formal or informal racial quota arrangements have seemed the logical compromises to settle these disputes. Federal agencies also have sanctioned quota systems in the past and have at least left the impression that they expect government contractors to give preferential treatment to minorities in filling these quotas. For example, one of the nondiscriminatory policies specified by the United States Department of Labor's apprenticeship training standards is "the taking of whatever steps are necessary, in acting upon application lists developed prior to this time, *to remove the effects of previous practices* under which discriminatory patterns of employment may have resulted" (emphasis added). Although the standards specifically bar quota systems, construction union critics of these standards insist that they contemplate preferential treatment in the selection of nonwhites. Some employers also argue that the standards for compliance with nondiscrimination clauses in government contracts strongly imply that preferential treatment should be given nonwhites in order to improve the manpower profiles which they are required to submit annually as "proof of affirmative action."

It would also be very unlikely that in the absence of preferential treatment nonwhite blue-collar employment by government contractors would have increased while total blue-collar employment was declining, as it has done in recent years. In addition, companies signing Plans for Progress with the President's Committee on Equal Employment Opportunity agree to "vigorously seek qualified minority group applicants for all job categories, and will make particular efforts to increase minority group representation in occupations at the higher levels of skill and responsibility." The Boeing Company, one of the prime contractors in the construction of the National Aeronautics and Space Administration's Michaud plant in New Orleans, announced in 1963 that it was importing Negro craftsmen from the North because it was bound by its government contract to "maintain balance between the races." [23]

Although quota systems seem to have been specifically banned by most state antidiscrimination commissions and by the NLRB, the Civil Rights Act of 1964 is not clear with respect to the legality of these practices. As noted earlier, the act merely declares that preferential treatment and quota systems *are not required by Title VII*. Presumably, preferential treatment could be legal, though not required. However, in order to be consistent with other provisions of the act, preferential treatment which discriminates against whites presumably would be unlawful, but preferential treatment which does not deprive whites of established rights would probably be lawful.

The National Labor Relations Board's decision in the Brownsville ILA case dealt with the legality of a racial quota system. In this case, which involved Locals 1367 (white) and 1368 (Negro) of the International Longshoremen's Association in Brownsville, Texas, the NLRB ruled that by maintaining a quota system which divided work 75–25 between Locals 1367 and 1368 "based on race and union membership" and by prohibiting Negro and white gangs from working together, the South Atlantic and Gulf Coast District of ILA and Local 1367 "failed to comply with their duty as exclusive bargaining representative to represent all employees in the bargaining unit fairly and impartially and thereby violated Section 8(b)(1)(A) of the Act." [24]

Quota systems have existed among Southern longshoremen since the Civil War, and have been buttressed by racially segregated local unions. On the Gulf and South Atlantic ports, many longshoremen's jobs have been held exclusively by Negroes, but in New Orleans and the Western Gulf ports there are segregated locals and racial quota systems. With few exceptions, clerks' jobs are held exclusively by whites. Negro longshoremen have been able to retain their positions mainly because they have had sufficient supplies of labor to prevent whites from freezing them out.

The Equal Employment Opportunity Commission (EEOC) raised the question of preferential treatment in a 1966 upgrading settlement at the Newport News Shipbuilding & Dry Dock Co., a Virginia-based Federal contractor, which the commission hopes will become a pattern for other industries. This agreement was entered into "voluntarily" by the company after the Labor Department threatened to cancel the firm's government contracts and the Justice Department was preparing to bring suit alleging a pattern of discrimination in violation of Title VII of the Civil Rights Act. The EEOC's investigations disclosed that although Negroes constituted 5,000 of the company's 19,000 employees, they held only 32 of 1,997 supervisory positions and only 6 of 506 apprenticeships. The settlement, which the company accepted to avoid litigation and possible loss of almost $5.5 billion in government contracts, provides for the appointment of an outside expert to supervise job evaluation, and upgrading and pay equalization programs for Negroes. The qualifications of the 100 newest supervisors will be studied and any Negro exceeding the qualifications of any of these supervisors will be placed on a preferential promotion list. The company was urged to see to it that "substantial numbers" of Negroes are included in new apprenticeship classes, and has agreed to give preferential treatment to qualified Negro applicants in selecting candidates for training programs. The agreement also provides for a study of white promotions and stipulates that "Upon establishment that a Negro employee has not moved up through the grades within the classification in which he is presently employed as rapidly as the norm or standard derived from the sample of white employees, he shall forthwith be assigned the first grade in his job classification, or such other grade as he would have achieved had his history followed the normal progression. . . ."

It remains to be seen, of course, if this agreement results in many Negroes being upgraded. Much depends upon the qualifications of the Negroes hired in the past, when it was not expected that they would be promoted to nontraditional jobs; the company's future manpower needs are another important factor. The agreement has also been challenged by the Penninsula Shipbuilders Association, an independent union representing workers at the company. The association alleges that the company's agreement with the EEOC violated its collective bargaining agreement by changing working conditions without consulting the union.

Preferential treatment for Negroes is opposed, of

course, because it might deprive whites of rights they already enjoy and therefore would be discrimination in reverse. But special programs for Negroes need not take the form of quota systems and need not deprive whites of existing rights. For example, employers and unions that have not recruited among Negroes in the past and that have no Negro employees or members might make special efforts to recruit Negroes or to help them acquire training. This would involve special efforts to include Negroes in the recruitment pattern, but it would not be preferential treatment because it would extend to Negroes benefits which whites already enjoy.

Even preferential treatment of Negroes can be conducted in such a way as not to deprive whites of existing rights. For example, if a Negro and a white applicant were about equally qualified, it would be preferential treatment if the Negro were hired in order to advertise to the Negro community (or government agencies) that the company had lowered its racial barriers. In this case the white applicant would not be deprived of pre-existing rights, although under the CRA he could presumably file a charge of discrimination against him because of his race. Of course, the form of preferential treatment that most critics apparently have in mind is the hiring of Negroes regardless of their qualifications when more qualified whites are available, or the actual displacement of whites by Negroes. The latter form of preferential treatment understandably leads to racial unrest.

The Problem of Tests

Because of their significance as determinants of whether or not Negroes get jobs or promotions, qualification tests become very important as formal racial barriers are lowered. Section 703(h) of the CRA provides that it shall not be unlawful for an employer "to give and to act upon the results of any professionally developed ability test provided that such test, its administration or action upon the results is not designed, intended or used to discriminate because of race, color, religion, sex, or national origin."

Senator John Tower (R., Tex.) inserted Section 703(h) as a qualification to Title VII in order to avoid the problem which arose in the *Myart v. Motorola, Inc.*, case in which a hearing examiner for the Illinois Fair Employment Practices Commission found that a Negro applicant for a job at Motorola had been discriminated against because the test did not "reflect and equate inequalities and environmental factors among the disadvantaged and culturally deprived groups." [25] Title VII makes it lawful for the employer to use a qualification test if there is no *intention* to discriminate, but does not address itself to the very important problem of whether or not these tests in fact do discriminate against Negroes or other persons similarly situated. Nor is it clear whether or not an employer gives evidence of bad faith and an intention to discriminate if he continues to administer a test which competent professionals find to be inherently discriminatory. Since professionals could presumably disagree over the validity of a test, the deciding criterion for purposes of Title VII undoubtedly will be intention to discriminate.

Is Title VII Likely to Change Racial Employment Patterns?

Assessment of Title VII's probable impact on racial employment patterns depends upon an evaluation of the adequacy of Title VII's procedures and power to prevent discrimination and of the law's ability to change those factors responsible for racial employment patterns. Although it is too early to say whether the EEOC's power is sufficient, many civil rights leaders seem convinced that the commission does not have adequate power, that the penalties need to be strengthened, and that the EEOC should be given power to initiate cases and issue cease and desist orders.

However, even if the CRA is strengthened, it probably will have only limited effects on racial employment patterns because the law is but one of the factors influencing employment patterns. The law is an important factor establishing the framework within which racial employment patterns *can be* changed, but it is not a significant factor determining the extent to which racial employment patterns *actually will* change. In other words, the law is a necessary but not a sufficient cause of significant changes in racial employment patterns. The law serves to create a favorable atmosphere for change by demonstrating the majority will and by putting bigots on the defensive, makes it possible to eliminate overt and blatant forms of discrimination, and, most important, gives those who are disposed not to discriminate an excuse for changing their ways. This latter is particularly important in unions where elected officials have permitted discrimination to continue for fear of their members' reactions to change. The law is also an important factor in overcoming employers' fears of adverse reactions to change by their white employees, their customers, and the community. Finally, the law might stimulate "voluntary" activities like the Plans for Progress, which, if backed by sanctions like government contract clauses and ultimate threats of prosecution under civil rights laws, can have a much greater effect than vigorous enforcement of Title VII. It is precisely because the "voluntary" plans can reach beyond the requirements of the law that they are likely to be more effective than mere law enforcement.

It can not be maintained either that the laws are unnecessary or that they alone can cause basic changes in employment patterns if they are vigorously enforced. Some observers who favor merit employment feel that legislation is unnecessary because the market tends to eliminate discrimination and because laws interfere with the employer's ability to make rational choices. Professor Milton Friedman, leading exponent of this view, argues that,

> It is a striking historical fact that the development of capitalism has been accompanied by a major reduction in the extent to which particular religious, racial, or social groups have operated under special handicaps in respect of their economic activities; have, as the saying goes, been discriminated against.

This is true because, according to Friedman,

> . . . there is an economic incentive in a free mar-
> ket to separate economic efficiency from other charac-
> teristics of the individual.[26]

Professor Friedman, therefore, believes that FEP legislation "clearly involves interference with the freedom of
individuals to enter into voluntary contracts with one another." If Professor Friedman is talking about an idealized
world which does not exist, one may grant his conclusions,
but if he means by "historical fact" that such an idealized
world exists, it is difficult to agree with him. Indeed, he
recognizes that employers might discriminate against Negroes not because of prejudice, but because they "may
simply be transmitting the tastes of the community." Thus,
in a perfectly rational economic world, it is possible that
noneconomic considerations like social pressures might
permanently counteract economic tendencies. Of course,
one might agree with Professor Friedman that the laws are
unnecessary if one lived in a world where

> . . . the appropriate recourse of those of us who
> believe that a particular criterion such as color is irrele-
> vant [was] to persuade our fellows to be of like mind,
> not to use the coercive power of the state to force
> them to act in accordance with our principles.[27]

But those who believe that rational discourse alone is not
likely to persuade many bigots to change their ways will
favor legislation to help achieve this end.

Narrow economic interpretations like those advanced
by Friedman fail to consider the social context within
which employment decisions are made. Economic forces—
like profit maximization—have predictive value in the real
world only if they are not counteracted by social forces
which make employers afraid to attempt profit maximization. Indeed, the law *facilitates* merit employment decisions by counteracting those social tendencies which prevent rational employment decisions. The laissez faire
position also fails to consider that the *rate* at which the
market tends to eliminate discrimination might be very
slow.

But although the laws are necessary, there is a real danger that their impact on employment will be exaggerated. Indeed, one of the reasons many civil rights leaders are disillusioned with the state FEP laws is because they assumed that the laws would cause significant changes in racial employment patterns. Employment patterns are not, however, determined mainly by the laws but, rather, by a host of factors, only one of which is discrimination. Changes in racial employment patterns are much more likely to respond to general expansion in employment, improvements in education and training, manpower policies to improve labor mobility, job forecasting, and employment counseling. Indeed, antidiscrimination legislation is likely to be most effective if it is considered as a part of general manpower and employment policies.

Those who argue for primary emphasis on vigorous law enforcement fail to consider some very basic limitations of laws as instruments of social change in a democracy. For instance, it is clear that preferential treatment for Negroes would cause changes in racial employment patterns more rapidly than would merely giving Negroes equal employment opportunities *from now on*. But it is equally clear that the law cannot *require* preferential treatment, because to do so would involve discrimination against whites. Similarly, it would seem to be a highly questionable legal procedure to use past discrimination as evidence of violations of Title VII. Obviously, moreover, patterns of racial imbalance cannot be considered illegal per se.

The foregoing is not meant to imply a criticism of special efforts by employers, unions, and employment agencies to correct racial imbalances—special efforts which do not deprive whites of pre-existing rights should be employed to correct racial imbalances. But it is highly doubtful that these special efforts should be *required* by law. Moreover, it seems obvious that these affirmative measures will be most effective under conditions of relatively full employment and an active labor market.

There are other features of the law which limit its

impact on employment patterns. For one thing, the requirements of due process often necessitate lengthy proceedings on individual complaints, limiting the number of people who can be affected. Moreover, the law can only prevent discrimination and does not touch the other cultural and social factors which influence an individual's knowledge of job opportunities and his willingness or ability to prepare himself for these jobs. Indeed, the fact that unequal job opportunities are due to other factors makes it difficult to prove the existence of discrimination in any particular case. It is equally clear, however, that the difficulties in proving racial discrimination in many cases make it possible for employers and unions to correct racial imbalances where they are motivated to do so.

In conclusion, the antidiscrimination laws are necessary parts of efforts to improve the operation of the labor market, but are much less important than general economic conditions in changing racial job patterns.

Chapter VIII

NEGRO-LABOR RELATIONS AND NEGRO JOB OPPORTUNITIES IN THE FUTURE

We have seen that Negro-labor relations were strained before the 1930's because of discrimination by unions, antiunion attitudes of Negro leaders, and the use of Negro strikebreakers. The AFL and many of its affiliates adopted nondiscrimination policies from the very beginning, but the federation's voluntary nature and the higher priority assigned other policies caused it to permit discrimination, particularly when the antiunion attitudes of the Negro community offered it some rationalization for those policies.

Because of the CIO's equalitarian racial position and because it appeared to be an emerging important power center, the Negro community became much more favorably disposed toward the new federation. For its part, the CIO needed Negro support to carry out its organizing and political objectives. While the CIO improved the Negro's position with unions and caused AFL unions to adopt more equalitarian positions, there was some discrimination by CIO rank-and-file members and local officers, especially in the South.

Negro-labor relations were exacerbated by certain features of the AFL-CIO merger and concomitant changes in the Negro community. AFL leaders (who were regarded with suspicion by many Negro leaders) gained control of the new federation. There were, moreover, many widely publicized cases of discrimination by AFL-CIO affiliates, and the Negroes' increased political power made them less dependent on unions. Negroes also were disillusioned because of the slow rate of improvement in, or actual deterioration of, their economic status relative to whites. Unions were considered to be at least partly responsible for the Negroes' economic disadvantages.

After a period of strained relations, union-Negro relations seem to have improved somewhat during the 1960's, at least at the national level, and the mutual objectives of unions and Negroes are likely to cause a continued cooperation between these groups. Negro-labor relations also were improved by the AFL-CIO's strong stand against racial discrimination, in unions as well as elsewhere, and its active support of civil rights legislation. This legislation, in turn, strengthened the federation's ability to deal with discrimination in its ranks. However, the persistence of discrimination at the local level, the differences in the priorities assigned civil rights objectives, and personality clashes between particular civil rights and union leaders, will cause tension to continue between these groups for some time.

Changes in Union Racial Practices

Since the 1930's notable changes have occurred in union racial practices. For one thing, the number of unions with formal race bars declined from at least 26 in 1930 to only 2 when the Civil Rights Act of 1964 outlawed these provisions. And even these two—the Locomotive Engineers and the Railway Conductors—had taken action to render their restrictive clauses inoperative where they conflicted with the laws. Auxiliary and segregated locals also were being rapidly abolished when they were made illegal by the CRA. There also had been important changes in the status of Negroes within unions. In the South, integrated locals were rare in 1930 but were very common in 1964. Moreover, total Negro union membership increased from about 56,000 in 1930 to over 1.5 million in 1964, and Negroes occupy official positions at practically every level.

The Negro's economic status also has changed markedly. Segregated seniority rosters have been eliminated in many places. A few Negroes have even moved into white-collar jobs and supervisory positions over whites in Southern plants—almost unheard of occurrences in 1930. Union protection has been extended to Negro workers in the form of seniority, grievance provisions, elimination of pay differentials, and improved fringe benefits. It is true that these changes have come about for trade union rather than racial reasons, but some unions have taken measures specifically designed to improve the positions of their Negro members and potential members.

Trade unions, of course, are not primarily responsible for these changes. No one who has carefully studied racial employment problems could conclude that any one factor has been responsible for reducing discrimination. Clearly, however, the single most important cause of these changes has been organized pressures from Negroes and from civil rights groups. But these pressures have been aided by a number of other factors, including: migration of Negroes into the unions' jurisdictions, especially during times of labor shortages; competition from nonunion Negro craftsmen; rivalry between unions for Negro support; legal action by the FEPC, the government contract committees, the courts, state FEP laws, and the NLRB; and the unions' need for Negro support in achieving political objectives.

There have, moreover, always been many American labor leaders who were opposed to discrimination because of moral reasons and because it clearly weakened the labor movement.

Although there have been these significant changes, there is no question that employment discrimination remains deeply imbedded in the labor movement, as well as in the rest of society. Even though almost all unions claim to be open to all qualified applicants, only token changes have taken place in many of the craft unions on the railroads and in the construction and printing industries. The exceptions to this generalization—such as IBEW Local 3 in New York—are insignificant compared with the number of local unions that have made no changes at all. Similarly, in spite of some formal changes and a few transfers of Negroes into previously all-white lines of progression in Southern plants, most Negroes remain in their traditional jobs. It is clear that in the absence of some really monumental developments, not many Negroes are likely to move into nontraditional jobs soon.

The obstacles to upgrading are numerous and include: (1) because of age or other considerations many Negroes will not elect to change jobs; (2) discrimination is difficult to prove, and unions have many reasons other than discrimination for vigorously resisting measures to get Negroes upgraded—these measures might upset seniority arrangements, which is always vigorously resisted; they might lead to demands for preferential treatment for Negroes, which also is likely to be resisted; (3) lengthy training times are required for many of these occupations; (4) employers and unions are likely to adopt qualifications and other standards which will be difficult for many Negroes to meet (and it is difficult to prove that these standards are discriminatory); (5) employment has been declining in many of the industries whose seniority rosters have been desegregated; (6) some qualified Negro craftsmen and contractors will not elect to be unionized because they have adequate job opportunities on a nonunion basis; and (7) many otherwise qualified Negro youngsters will go to college rather than into apprenticeship training programs.

However, enough experience has been accumulated in recent years to provide a pretty good idea of the kinds of things that have to be done to cause greater changes in employment structures. Most important, it is now clear that the barriers to Negro upgrading are so many, complex, and highly interrelated, that a massive attack has to be launched simultaneously on a number of fronts. A mere listing of the major factors necessary to accomplish this objective demonstrates the complexity of the problem: Negroes must be able to learn about job openings, be motivated to prepare themselves for these jobs, be able to acquire the necessary training, be able to get the jobs once they are trained, be admitted to unions which represent the workers in these jobs, and be able to advance on the job according to their qualifications and to participate in the unions on an equal basis.

One of the things essential to the achievement of these results is the creation of manpower and employment programs to increase the demand for labor and improve the operation of the labor market. Antidiscrimination legislation needs to be perfected and considered a part of overall manpower policies. Manpower policies should include the creation of jobs for specific groups, improved labor market information, and better counseling and guidance. It seems especially important to improve the job information available to Negro and other disadvantaged youngsters.

Civil rights legislation will have to be perfected and made a part of overall manpower policies. In particular, strategies must be devised to change the deeply entrenched practices of many unions and employers. Clearly, for example, intransigent local craft unions are not likely to respond to threats of public hearing and bad publicity; experience shows that these organizations will change their practices only when their control of jobs is threatened or when they are fined for noncompliance with administrative or court orders. It remains to be seen if any of the existing civil rights legislation will be able to address itself to this problem. Perhaps the international unions will be sufficiently convinced that their locals' traditional job control procedures are at stake to take action against their recalcitrant affiliates. It also remains to be seen if existing agencies can adopt standards and procedures to prevent unrealistic qualifications, unfair testing procedures, and subterfuges in the processing of applications, all of which are means of excluding Negroes from jobs, unions, and training programs.

It might also be helpful if compliance review programs were adopted which would require unions, employers, joint apprenticeship, and other training programs to report statistics by race. There was perhaps some excuse for prohibiting records by race when there were no antidiscrimination laws; now, however, the statistics which such records could provide are necessary for the adequate enforcement of the laws.

In addition, Congress would strengthen the NLRB's power to combat discrimination if it specifically removed the doubt in the Hughes Tool doctrine and made discrimination an unfair labor practice. The duty of fair representation also should be clarified and the employer should be made jointly liable for it. The NLRB's expertise would seem to give it some advantages in dealing with employment discrimination in unionized industries.

Finally, it has been learned that the nature of this problem is such that it cannot be remedied by law enforcement programs alone. Since the requirements of due process make law enforcement a very slow process in cases of racial discrimination, increased reliance should be placed on voluntary programs, which would, of course, not relieve respondents of any legal obligations or permit them in any way to evade the law. But employers and unions can do things voluntarily that they cannot be required to do by law.

Moreover, private groups like the NAACP and the Urban League play very important roles in supplementing legal programs. They can intensify their complaint gathering activities and do the detailed follow-up work necessary for the successful resolution of most cases. Civil rights organizations also can search the Negro community for qualified Negro applicants for various programs, and see that applicants follow up until they gain successful entry into jobs or training programs. Civil rights groups also might supply guidance and counseling to ensure successful completion of training programs or successful performance on jobs. This kind of detailed case work is especially important in dealing with young Negro workers who might not understand the necessary procedures involved, might be easily discouraged by delays and subterfuges, and often lack the discipline necessary for successful performance or completion of training. These organizations could also intensify their training activities to prepare youngsters to meet the qualifications necessary for entrance into various programs. It is especially important to give young Negroes experience with the kinds of tests they will be required to take.

The role of unions and employers in this process is too obvious to require further elaboration. The national unions have a particular responsibility in eradicating discrimination by their locals or in seeing to it that the locals supply enough information about their activities to remove the suspicion of discrimination. Ideally, of course, unions at every level would take affirmative action to actively seek out Negro applicants, as IBEW Local 3 did in New York. But, since this suggestion clashes with the monopoly instincts of many craft unions, it is probable that only a few of them will follow Local 3's lead. It will therefore be necessary for other organizations to supply the qualified applicants. Indeed, since most unions declare themselves open to all qualified persons, one of the best ways to test their sincerity (and perfect techniques to change their practices if they are discriminating), is to produce the qualified people. And international unions probably will not take action to get more Negroes into their locals unless they have evidence that qualified persons have been barred.

The Prospects

A preoccupation with union racial practices should not be allowed to obscure the fact that more and better jobs should be the real end of public policy. It is, consequently, essential to examine the overall prospects for improving the job opportunities for Negroes.

Although it is not possible to strike a precise balance, some current trends clearly stimulate and others retard the income and employment positions of Negroes. The favorable factors include:

1. The Negro's political power has increased as he migrates out of the rural South. Although this process will continue, it will be relatively less important in the future because only about 10 percent of the nonwhite workforce remains in farming. At the same time, however, the prospects are that the Negroes' political power will continue to increase because of expanding voting rights, and other changes in the South. As a result, Negro employment by Southern state and local governments probably will increase relatively rapidly in the next twenty years and will continue to increase rapidly in the skilled and white-collar categories of employment by the Federal Government and its contractors. Negroes who acquire experience in the Federal service will probably be able to move into better jobs in the private sector. It is even likely that antidiscrimination legislation will be adopted by a number of Southern municipalities.

2. One of the most optimistic features of the recent racial employment experience has been the apparent commitment by the nation's major employers to more equalitarian employment practices. In part, this is because employers have been freed by public policies from social pressures which perpetuate job discrimination. But the employers' commitment also is due to a growing realization that the mood of the Negro community is such that demonstrations and pressure on the Federal Government will continue until racial barriers are lowered. The South-

ern business community has belatedly responded to these civil rights pressures and is using its considerable influence to moderate the extremists. To a considerable extent, however, these changes also result from the growing industrialization of the South, which tends to draw the South increasingly into the mainstream of the American economy.

3. The civil rights movement has strengthened equalitarian forces within the labor movement and has caused racial matters to have much higher priority in the AFL-CIO than they had in either the CIO or the AFL. Antidiscrimination legislation makes it easier for the AFL-CIO Civil Rights Department to fight discrimination within the labor movement, and the federation's civil rights machinery has been invigorated since 1960; moreover, Negro union members have become better organized to promote their own interests within the unions. It also can be expected that the increasing power of the civil rights movement, which lessens the movement's dependence on unions, will be a pressure on discriminating unions. The civil rights and labor movements' mutual political interests probably will continue to be a significant force for improving the Negro's economic position.

4. The Civil Rights Act of 1964, the state antidiscrimination laws, NLRB doctrines, and court decisions form an impressive array of public policy measures to combat discrimination. Since civil rights organizations have become institutionalized and need to demonstrate results in order to survive and grow in competition with each other, there can be little doubt that these public policies will be perfected as instruments to combat discrimination.

5. The trend toward improvement in the quality and amount of education of nonwhites undoubtedly will improve the Negro's economic position. There is already some evidence, for example, that a major obstacle to increasing the number of Negroes in the professional and technical categories is the absence of qualified candidates. Federal aid and the elimination of discrimination are likely to improve the quality of the education received by Negroes in the South. Indeed, just as the Negro is currently handi-

capped by the cumulative effects of inferior training, so education and training together promise to be the Negro's single most important avenue of advancement.

6. The trend towards an active Federal manpower policy will undoubtedly help Negroes by providing better job training and improved counseling and information services. There is an obvious need, however, to coordinate antidiscrimination and manpower policies. Although the MDTA, ARA, and poverty programs have not had very much effect on Negro job opportunities, as these policies are perfected they will undoubtedly be instruments to improve the racial job patterns. A really effective labor market might even facilitate the dispersion of Negroes from the ghettos, which currently exert harmful pressures on training and employment. Clearly, however, an effective manpower policy must contemplate the creation of jobs to fit workers as well as workers to fit projected jobs.

Counteracting these favorable factors are a number of others that will impede the rate of improvement in Negro job patterns:

1. Although there have been some *relatively* significant breakthroughs in employment discrimination, in an absolute sense discrimination is still a very important obstacle to Negro job improvement. While measures can be taken to reduce discrimination, racial prejudices are likely to persist for a long time. In spite of a few cases of very significant developments in the last ten years, most of the breakthroughs in the skilled trades can hardly be classified as more than token changes, and it is still too early to determine whether these changes will remain in the token category or whether they will be converted into significant increases in the numbers of skilled Negro craftsmen.

It is likely, however, that efforts by Negroes to break into the building trades unions from which they have been barred will continue to be a controversial problem for a long time. The craft union problem is difficult because of local autonomy, nepotism, the economic power of these unions, and the members' fear that the time and resources invested in developing their crafts will be sacrificed because of preferential treatment for Negroes. This problem also is aggravated by what craft unionists conceive to be limited job opportunities which must be conserved for their members. The most effective measures to improve the Negroes' job patterns therefore are likely to be those which reassure workers in the buffer zone between the professional and technical jobs, where there is increasing demand, and the less skilled categories where demand is static or declining and opportunities are limited for whites as well as Negroes.

2. Another unfavorable factor for Negro employment prospects is the very great amount of effort which has been required to produce additional jobs. The disappointing results produced by the state antidiscrimination laws was due in part to this difficulty and to the misconception that lowering the racial barriers would in and of itself produce significant job changes. To a very significant extent, of course, the Negro's job problems are due to factors other than current discrimination, because if all Negroes were made white tomorrow it would be a long time before Negroes overcame the impact of their cultural disadvantages, which have caused poor work habits, inadequate motivation, and ignorance of job requirements and availability.

3. Since nondiscrimination policies have been developed and can expect to be perfected, the Negroes' job conditions in the future are likely to be conditioned more by the level of employment than by specific antidiscrimination measures. Since unemployment declines faster for nonwhites than for whites and Negro male employment increases faster than white male employment in expanding industries, and since full employment would sweep away many of the obstacles imposed by whites to Negro employment opportunities, the most important things that can be done to promote economic opportunities for Negroes are those things which would achieve full employment and economic growth. Although unemployment declined below the 4 percent level during 1966, it remains to be seen if

unemployment can be maintained at such a low level for a sustained period of time.

In conclusion, therefore, the Negro's prospects for equal job opportunities are good, but it means very little to get an equal share of inadequate jobs. Really significant changes in the racial job patterns will require rapid economic growth and measures to maintain full employment coordinated with active labor market policies which include antidiscrimination measures. These labor market, full employment, and economic growth measures must work against great obstacles, and therefore, while the Negro's job position is likely to continue to improve absolutely, Negro-white income and employment gaps are likely to close too slowly to keep these issues from remaining important domestic problems for many years.

Notes

CHAPTER I

1. W. J. Cash, *The Mind of the South* (New York: Knopf, 1941), p. 107.
2. See Marcus Jernigan, *Laboring and Dependent Classes in Colonial America* (Chicago: University of Chicago Press, 1931).
3. Quoted by Kenneth M. Stampp, *The Peculiar Institution* (New York: Knopf, 1956), p. 427.
4. R. B. Morris, "Labor Militancy in the Old South," *Labor and Nation*, Vol. 1, No. 5 (May–June 1948), p. 33.
5. Sterling D. Spero and Abram L. Harris, *The Black Worker* (New York: Columbia University Press, 1931), p. 11.
6. *Ibid.*
7. Gunnar Myrdal, with the assistance of Richard Sterner and Arnold Rose, *An American Dilemma* (New York: Harper & Row, 1944), p. 1101.
8. E. Franklin Frazier, *The Negro Family in the United States* (Chicago: University of Chicago Press, 1939), p. 447.
9. See Myrdal, *op. cit.*, p. 1965.
10. C. Vann Woodward, *The Burden of Southern History* (New York: Random House, 1961), Chap. 5; John H. Franklin, *Reconstruction After the Civil War* (Chicago:

University of Chicago Press, 1962); and Myrdal, *op. cit.*, p. 446.

11. C. Vann Woodward, *Strange Career of Jim Crow* (New York: Oxford University Press, 1957), p. 40.

12. Vernon L. Wharton, *The Negro in Mississippi, 1877–1880* (Chapel Hill: University of North Carolina Press, 1947) and George B. Tendall, *South Carolina Negroes, 1877–1880* (Chapel Hill: University of North Carolina Press, 1952).

13. Charles H. Wesley, *Negro Labor in the United States* (New York: Vanguard, 1927), p. 112.

14. John R. Commons, ed., *Trade Unionism and Labor Problems* (Boston: Ginn, 1905), p. 364.

CHAPTER II

1. John R. Commons and Associates, eds., *A Documentary History of American Industrial Society*, Vol. IX (Cleveland: Arthur H. Clark Co., 1910), p. 159.

2. Quoted by Philip Taft, *Organized Labor in American History* (New York: Harper & Row, 1964), p. 91.

3. Sterling D. Spero and Abram L. Harris, *The Black Worker* (New York: Columbia University Press, 1931), pp. 24, 40–45; H. M. Douty, "Early Labor Organizations in North Carolina," *South Atlantic Quarterly*, Vol. 34, No. 3 (July 1935), p. 262; Frederic Meyers, "Knights of Labor in the South," *Southern Economic Journal*, Vol. VI, No. 4 (April 1940), p. 479; George S. Mitchell, *Textile Unionism and the South* (Chapel Hill: University of North Carolina Press, 1931), pp. 23–24; Holman Head, "Development of the Labor Movement in Alabama Prior to 1900," unpublished M.A. thesis, University of Alabama, 1954; and Ruth A. Allen, *Chapters in the History of Organized Labor in Texas* (Austin: University of Texas Press, 1941), p. 174.

4. AFL *Convention Proceedings* (1895), p. 69.

5. AFL *Convention Proceedings* (1900), pp. xiii, 12–13.

6. Booker T. Washington, "The Negro and the Labor Unions," *Atlantic Monthly* (June 1913), p. 756.

7. John P. Frey, "Attempts to Organize Negro Workers," *American Federationist*, Vol. 36 (March 1929), p. 297.

8. AFL *Executive Council Minutes* (February 10–17, 1917).

9. *Ibid.*

10. Calvin B. Hoover and B. U. Ratchford, *Economic Resources and Policies of the South* (New York: Macmillan,

1951), p. 20 and 1964 estimate from U. S. Bureau of the Census figures.

11. See Gunnar Myrdal, *An American Dilemma* (New York: Harper & Row, 1944), p. 567 and Chicago Commission on Racial Relations, *The Negro in Chicago* (Chicago: University of Chicago Press, 1922), pp. 67–72.

12. Personal interview with George Googe, AFL-CIO Southern Representative from 1928–48 (Atlanta, Georgia, April 12, 1959).

13. UMW *Convention Proceedings* (1942), p. 189.

14. Irving Howe and B. J. Widick, *The UAW and Walter Reuther* (New York: Harper & Row, 1948), p. 218 and Walter Galenson, *The CIO Challenge to the AFL* (Cambridge, Mass.: Harvard University Press, 1960), pp. 180–181.

15. CIO *Convention Proceedings* (1952), p. 367.

16. "Negroes War," *Fortune*, Vol. XXV, No. 6 (June 1942), pp. 77–80, 157–164.

17. Report of the Director, Committee to Abolish Discrimination (November 18, 1950); Committee to Abolish Discrimination *Minutes* (May 25, 1943 and October 26, 1949); Committee to Abolish Discrimination *Report* (November 1946); and Committee to Abolish Discrimination *Minutes* (May 12, 1945).

18. Ira de A. Reid, *Negro Membership in Labor Unions* (New York: National Urban League, 1930).

19. Abram L. Harris, *The Negro Worker* (New York: Conference for Progressive Labor Action, 1930).

20. Jessie P. Guzman, *The Negro Year Book* (Tuskegee, Ala.: Tuskegee Institute, 1947); see also George F. McCrary, "The Labor Movement, 1944–1945," in Florence Murray, ed., *The Negro Handbook* (New York: Current Books, 1947), p. 109.

CHAPTER III

1. AFL-CIO *Convention Proceedings* (1955), pp. 363, 387.

2. *Chicago Defender* (February 19, 1955), p. 1.

3. AFL-CIO *Convention Proceedings* (1955), pp. 305–308.

4. *Ibid.*

5. *Pittsburgh Courier* (December 17, 1955), p. 9.

6. *Chicago Defender* (December 3, 1955), p. 4.

7. *Chicago Defender* (June 1, 1957), p. 1 and *Fortune*, Vol. LIX, No. 3 (March 11, 1959), pp. 191–194.

8. National Association for the Advancement of Colored People, Labor Department, "Racism Within Organized Labor: A Report of Five Years of the AFL-CIO, 1955–1960," mimeographed, pp. 2–3.

9. Memorandum to Boris Shishkin, Director, Civil Rights Department, AFL-CIO, from Herbert Hill, Labor Secretary, NAACP (December 4, 1958).

10. James Jones, quoted in *Greater Philadelphia Magazine* (February 1963), p. 1.

11. AFL-CIO *Proceedings, Fifth Day,* Third Constitutional Convention (1959), p. 130.

12. This version of Meany's reply is taken from the writer's personal notes. The official version printed in the *Proceedings* is substantially the same, but reads: "Who appointed you as guardian. . . ?"

13. See, for example, Baltimore *Afro-American* (October 24, 1959), p. 1 and *Pittsburgh Courier* (October 10, 1959), p. 1.

14. Confidential letter to the writer (April 30, 1962).

15. See, for example, *The New York Times* (November 12, 1962), p. 23.

16. *Jet* (November 16, 1961), pp. 16–20.

17. *The New York Times* (November 12, 1961), p. 1.

18. *Ibid.*

19. Confidential letter to Ray Marshall from AFL-CIO official (April 30, 1962).

20. *The New York Times* (November 12, 1962), p. 5.

21. Statement in *Jet* (November 16, 1961), p. 21.

22. Reported by Tom Brooks, "The Negro's Place at Labor's Table," *The Reporter,* Vol. 27, No. 10 (December 6, 1962), p. 39.

23. *The New York Times* (November 12, 1962), p. 5 and *AFL-CIO News* (November 17, 1962).

24. Letter to the writer from Emil Schlesinger (March 17, 1964), and *Justice* (June 1, 1963), p. 1.

25. *The New York Times* (May 18, 1965), p. 12.

26. *Labor Today,* Vol. 22 (Spring 1962), p. 12.

27. See Herbert Hill, " 'Right to Work' Laws and the Negro Workers," *The Crisis,* Vol. 64, No. 6 (July 1957) and "Randolph Urges Negroes to Repudiate 'Work' Law," *AFL-CIO News* (February 22, 1964), p. 11.

CHAPTER IV

1. See Ray Marshall, "Union Racial Problems in the South," *Industrial Relations,* Vol. 1, No. 3 (May 1962), pp. 117-128.
2. USEA, *Independent Trade Union News* (no date).
3. Letter to the writer from Harry W. Brown, President of USEA (June 4, 1959).
4. *Charlotte* (N. C.) *Observer* (September 1 and 2, 1957), p. 1.
5. Advertisement published in the public interest by Southern Crafts, Inc., in *South* (June 17, 1957).
6. *Ibid.*
7. Copy of SSCUP resolution in Ray Marshall's possession (no date).
8. *Chattanooga* (Tenn.) *Times* (July 1, 1956), p. 1.
9. *News-Free Press* (Chattanooga, Tenn., August 3 and 20, 1955) and *Chattanooga Times* (August 21, 1955). For a more detailed discussion see Marshall, *op. cit.*
10. RWDSU *Record* (January 12, 1964), p. 9.

CHAPTER V

1. Abram L. Harris, in *The Negro Worker* (New York: Conference for Progressive Labor Action, 1930), p. 8, listed the following AFL unions with formal race bars in 1930:
    1. Brotherhood of Railway Carmen (BRC)
    2. The Switchmen's Union of North America (SNA)
    3. The Order of Sleeping Car Conductors (OSCC)
    4. The [International] National Organization of Masters, Mates and Pilots of North America (MMP)
    5. The Railway Mail Association (RMA)
    6. American Wire Weavers Protective Association (WWPA)
    7. Commercial Telegraphers (CT)
    8. The Boilermakers, Iron Shipbuilders and Helpers Union (BIS)
    9. The Order of Railway [Railroad] Telegraphers (ORT)
    10. The International Association of Machinists (IAM)

11. Brotherhood of Railway and Steamship Clerks (BRSC)

Harris listed the following unaffiliated unions as having race bars in 1930:

1. American Federation of Express Workers (AFEW)
2. American Federation of Railway Workers (AFRW)
3. Brotherhood of Railway Station Employees and Clerks (BRSEC)
4. [American] Train Dispatchers [Association] (ATDA)
5. Railroad Yard Masters of America (RYA)
6. Neptune Association (NA)
7. Brotherhood of Locomotive Engineers (BLE)
8. Brotherhood [Order?] of Railway Conductors (ORC)
9. Brotherhood of Locomotive Firemen and Enginemen (BLFE)
10. Brotherhood of Railroad Trainmen (BRT)
11. Order of Railway Telegraphers (ORT)
12. Brotherhood of Dining Car Conductors (BDCC)
13. Order of Railway Expressmen (ORE)

Harris said that there were 26 unions with racial bars, 10 of which were AFL affiliates, though he listed only 24 unions, 11 of which were AFL affiliates. The U. S. Department of Labor, Bureau of Labor Statistics, in its 1926 *Handbook of American Trade Unions* listed the following unions with race bars: BDCC, AFRW, ORE, AFREW, BRSEC, RYA, the Railroad Yard Masters of North America (RYNA), NA, BRT, ORC, BLE, and BLFE. In addition, Spero and Harris, *The Black Worker* (New York: Columbia University Press, 1931), p. 57, listed the following AFL organizations with race bars in 1929, which also probably had race bars in 1926: BRC, SNA, BRSC, CT, OSCC, ORT, MMP, RMA, WWPA, BIS, and the IAM. Between 1926 and 1930, however, the ORE and the AFEW returned to the BRSC, and in 1929 the BRSE no longer limited membership to whites. Thus, Spero and Harris concluded, "in 1930 there are nine unions affiliated with the Federation and ten unaffiliated unions whose constitutions debar Negro members." (*Ibid.*, p. 58.)

2. BLE *Constitution* of June–July, 1956, as amended September 1960, Section 28.

3. BLFE *Constitution* of July–August, 1959, as amended January 8, 1960.

4. See Mark Perlman, *The Machinists* (Cambridge, Mass.: Harvard University Press, 1961), Chap. 1.

5. Harry Henig, *The Brotherhood of Railway Clerks* (New York: Columbia University Press, 1937), *passim*.

6. AFL *Executive Council Minutes* (September 30 and October 10, 1940), p. 133.

7. AFL *Convention Proceedings* (1940), p. 649.

8. FEPC *Final Report* (1946), p. 20.

9. Malcolm Ross, *All Manner of Men* (New York: Reynal & Hitchcock, 1947), p. 147.

10. Robert Weaver, *Negro Labor* (New York: Harcourt, Brace, 1946), pp. 228–229.

11. See James *v.* Marinship, 25 Calif. 2d 721 (1944).

12. IAM *Executive Council Minutes* (September 21–26, 1925; December 3–12, 1940; December 1–13, 1941; July 18–24, 1941; and June 26–31, 1942).

13. *Congressional Record,* 78th Cong., 1st Sess., Vol. 89, No. 65, p. 1245.

14. Texas Motor Freight Lines, Hearing Case No. 16-R-2223 (April 9, 1943), pp. 32–33.

15. Arnold M. Rose, *Union Solidarity* (Minneapolis: University of Minnesota Press, 1952), Chap. 5.

16. N. Y. City Commission on Human Rights, *Bias in the Building Industry, An Interim Report to the Mayor* (December 13, 1963), p. 10.

17. *Ibid.,* pp. 11–12.

18. *Electrical Workers* (April 1903), p. 102.

19. IBEW *Proceedings,* Eighth Biennial Convention, President's Report (1905), p. 18.

20. IBEW Executive Board *Proceedings* (January 27–February 11, 1905).

21. IBEW *Proceedings,* 1927 Convention, p. 25.

22. Connecticut Supplement (1952), pp. 125–127; *Connecticut Law Journal* (October 7, 1952), p. 2; IBEW Local 35 *v.* Commission on Civil Rights, Conn. Supreme Court of Errors (October term, 1953); and IBEW Local 35 *v.* Commission on Civil Rights, Superior Court, Hartford County, Conn., File No. 90352 (March 26, 1954).

23. Letter to Ray Marshall from Peter E. Terzick, UBCJ General Treasurer (March 4, 1964).

24. *Ibid.*

25. Letter to George Meany from James C. Petrillo (April 8, 1958).

26. AFM *Proceedings,* Sixteenth Annual Convention (1957), p. 82.
27. Letter from Petrillo to Meany (April 8, 1958).
28. Letter to Ray Marshall (March 4, 1964).

CHAPTER VI

1. 88th Cong., 2d Sess., Joint Economic Committee, *Joint Economic Report* (1964), Senate Report No. 931, p. 61.
2. *Report of the President's Committee on Equal Employment Opportunity* (1963), p. 34.
3. Negroes constituted 17 percent of the total increase in Federal employment between 1961 and 1962 and 22 percent of the increase between 1962 and 1963. In 1963 there were 302,000 Negro employees in the Federal service. Between 1962 and 1963 Negroes increased their proportion of GS–5 through GS–11 jobs by 14.7 percent while the total increased by 5.1 percent and by 38.7 percent in GS–12 through GS–18 jobs as compared with a total of 12.4 percent.
4. *Manpower Report of the President* (1964), p. 201.
5. Dale E. Hiestand, *Economic Growth and Employment Opportunities of Minorities* (New York: Columbia University Press, 1964), pp. 110–111.
6. *Manpower Report of the President* (1964), p. 99.
7. Statement of Samuel Ganz, Assistant Director for Manpower and Automation Research, Office of Manpower, Automation and Training, U. S. Department of Labor, to the U. S. Senate Subcommittee on Employment and Manpower of the Committee on Labor and Public Welfare (September 10, 1963).
8. *Statistical Abstract of the United States* (1964), p. 230.
9. Statement by Sar Levitan, "Training Under the Area Redevelopment Act," to the U. S. Senate Employment and Manpower Subcommittee (June 7, 1963).
10. Letter to Ray Marshall from Howard Rosen, Assistant Director for Manpower and Automation Research, U. S. Department of Labor (November 13, 1964) and 1966 *Report of the Secretary of Labor on Research and Training* under the MDTA.
11. George P. Schultz, "The Fort Worth Project of the Armour Automation Committee," *Monthly Labor Review,* Vol. 87, No. 1 (January 1964), p. 56.
12. *Manpower Report of the President* (1964), p. 70.

13. J. J. Morrow, "American Negroes, A Wasted Resource," *Harvard Business Review*, Vol. 32, No. 1 (January–February, 1957), p. 69.
14. Connecticut Commission on Civil Rights, *Training of Negroes in Skilled Trades* (1954).
15. Irving Babow and Edward Howden, "Employment," in *A Civil Rights Inventory of San Francisco*, Part I (San Francisco: Council for Civic Unity of San Francisco, 1959), p. 109.
16. Langston T. Hawley, "Negro Employment in the Birmingham Metropolitan Area," Case Study No. 3, in *Selected Studies of Negro Employment in the South*, Report No. 6 (National Planning Association, Committee of the South, February 1963).
17. E. William Noland and E. Wight Bakke, *Workers Wanted: A Study of Employer Hiring Policies, Preferences, and Practices* (New York: Harper & Row, 1949), p. 59.
18. *Ibid.*, p. 32.
19. Bernard Rosenberg and Penny Chapin, "Management and Minority Groups: A Study of Attitudes and Practices in Hiring and Upgrading," in *Discrimination and Low Incomes* (New York: State Commission Against Discrimination, 1949).
20. Donald Dewey, "4 Studies of Negro Employment in the Upper South," Case Study Number 2 in *Selected Studies of Negro Employment in the South*, pp. 190–194.
21. Leon E. Lunden, "Antidiscrimination Provisions in Major Contracts, 1961," *Monthly Labor Review*, Vol. 86, No. 6 (June 1963), p. 643.

CHAPTER VII

1. Act of June 27, 1944, 58 Stat. 387, Independent Offices Appropriations Act of 1945, 31 USC 696.
2. Letter from Vice-President Nixon to all contracting agencies (May 4, 1957).
3. *Ibid.*
4. *The New York Times* (February 3, 1965), p. 22.
5. *The New York Times* (January 2, 1964), p. 37.
6. *Reports on Apprenticeship* (January 1964), p. 13.
7. *Ibid.*
8. Report to the President, The President's Committee on Equal Employment Opportunity (November 1963), p. 116.
9. PCEEO, Committee Reporter (November 1963).

10. *The New York Times* (December 19, 1963), p. 16.
11. See Ray Marshall, "Some Factors Influencing the Up-grading of Negroes in the Southern Petroleum Refining Industry," *Social Forces,* Vol. 42, No. 2 (December 1963) pp. 186–195.
12. U. S. Senate, Subcommittee on Manpower and Employ-ment, *Hearings on the Nation's Manpower Revolution,* Part 9 (1963), pp. 3134–3145.
13. See Paul Norgren and Samuel Hill, *Toward Fair Employ-ment* (New York: Columbia University Press, 1964).
14. *Ibid.*
15. Steele *v.* L. & N. R. R., 323 U. S. 192; Archibald Cox, "The Duty of Fair Representation," *Villanova Law Review* (January 1957); Benjamin Aaron, "Some Aspects of the Union's Duty of Fair Representation," *Ohio State Law Journal* (Winter 1961), p. 39; and Wallace Corp. *v.* NLRB, 323 U. S. 248.
16. Central of Georgia Ry. *v.* Jones, 229 F. 2d 648, Cert. denied 352 U. S. 848; Richardson *v.* Texas & New Orleans Ry. Co., 242 F. 2d 230; and 77 S.Ct.230.
17. See Syres *v.* Oil Workers 257 F. 2d 479; 330 U. S. 892; and Rolax *v.* Atlantic Coast Line 186 F. 2d 473.
18. NLRB, *Tenth Annual Report* (1945), p. 18.
19. 147 NLRB no. 166.
20. 140 NLRB no. 181.
21. 55 LRRM no. 2,715.
22. Local Union No. 12, United Rubber Workers and Business League of Gadsden, 150 NLRB No. 18.
23. *The New York Times* (July 13, 1963), p. 7.
24. Local 1367, ILA, Case No. 23–CB–467, 148 NLRB No. 44 (September 14, 1964).
25. See *Congressional Record* (March 19, 1964), for the Motorola decision. In the Motorola case, the company did not place the pre-employment intelligence test in evidence because the original tests were destroyed. It did, however, offer the applicant's test score as evidence. The hearing examiner's decision was later modified by the Illinois FEPC, which found it unnecessary to pass on the validity of the test.
26. Milton Friedman, *Capitalism and Freedom* (Chicago: University of Chicago Press, 1962), pp. 108–109.
27. *Ibid.,* p. 109.

Selected Bibliography

Bailer, Lloyd H. "Organized Labor and Racial Minorities: Recent Developments Affecting Union Policies." *Annals of the American Academy of Political and Social Science* (March 1951), pp. 101–107.

——. "The Negro Automobile Worker." *Journal of Political Economy* (October 1943), pp. 415–428.

Batchelder, Alan. "Decline in the Relative Income of Negro Men." *Quarterly Journal of Economics,* Vol. LXXVIII, No. 4 (November 1964), pp. 525–548.

Becker, Gary S. *The Economics of Discrimination.* Chicago: University of Chicago Press, 1957.

Cash, W. J. *The Mind of the South.* New York: Alfred A. Knopf, 1941.

Cayton, Horace, and Mitchell, George S. *Black Workers and New Unions.* Chapel Hill: University of North Carolina Press, 1939.

Committee of the South, The National Planning Association. *Selected Studies of Negro Employment in the South.* Washington, D.C.: National Planning Association, 1955.

Conant, James Bryant. *Slums and Suburbs.* New York: McGraw-Hill, 1961.

Dabbs, James McBride. *The Southern Heritage.* New York: Alfred A. Knopf, 1959.

Daniel, Walter G., ed. *The Relative Progress of the American Negro Since 1950.* Washington, D.C.: The Howard University Press, for the Bureau of Education Research, Howard

University, Yearbook Number of the Journal of Negro Education, Fall 1963.

Fein, Rashi. *An Economic and Social Profile of the Negro American,* Reprint 110. Washington, D.C.: The Brookings Institution, 1966.

Franklin, John W. *From Slavery to Freedom: A History of American Negroes.* New York: Alfred A. Knopf, 1956.

Garfinkel, Herbert. *When Negroes March.* Glencoe, Ill.: The Free Press, 1959.

Ginzberg, Eli. *The Negro Potential.* New York: Columbia University Press, 1956.

Greene, Lorenzo J., and Woodson, Carter G. *The Negro Wage Earner.* Washington, D.C.: Association for the Study of Negro Life and History, 1930.

Hiestand, Dale L. *Economic Growth and Employment Opportunities for Minorities.* New York: Columbia University Press, 1964.

Hope, II, John. *Equality of Opportunity, A Union Approach to Fair Employment.* Washington, D.C.: Public Affairs Press, 1956.

————. *Three Southern Plants of International Harvester Co.* Washington, D.C.: NPA, 1953.

————. "Current Minority Policies and their Implementation in International Unions." *American Journal of Economics and Sociology,* Vol. X (July 1951), pp. 371–388.

Kesselman, L. C. *The Social Politics of FEPC: A Study in Reform Pressure Movements.* Chapel Hill: University of North Carolina Press, 1948, p. 253.

Marshall, Ray. *The Negro and Organized Labor.* New York: John Wiley & Sons, 1965.

Mendelson, Wallace. *Discrimination.* Englewood Cliffs, N.J.: Prentice-Hall, 1962.

Mitchell, George S., and Cayton, Horace R. *Black Workers and the New Unions.* Chapel Hill: University of North Carolina Press, 1939.

Myrdal, Gunnar. *An American Dilemma.* New York: Harper & Row, 1944.

National Urban League. *Negro Membership in American Labor Unions.* New York: Department of Research and Investigation, 1930.

New York City Commission on Human Rights. *Bias in the Building Industry.* New York, 1963.

New York State Commission Against Discrimination. *Ap-*

prentices, Skilled Craftsmen and the Negro: An Analysis. New York, 1960.

Norgren, Paul H., and Samuel E. Hill, with the assistance of F. Ray Marshall. *Toward Fair Employment.* New York: Columbia University Press, 1964.

Norgren, Paul H., Albert N. Webster, Roger D. Borgeson, and Maud B. Patten, *Employing the Negro in American Industry.* New York: Industrial Relations Counselors, 1959.

Northrup, Herbert. *Organized Labor and the Negro.* New York: Harper & Row, 1944.

———, and Richard L. Rowan, eds. *The Negro and Employment Opportunity.* Ann Arbor: Bureau of Industrial Relations, University of Michigan, 1965.

Phillips, Ulrich B. *Life and Labor in the Old South.* New York: Little, Brown, 1929.

Record, C. Wilson. *The Negro and the Communist Party.* Chapel Hill: University of North Carolina Press, 1951.

Ross, Malcolm. *All Manner of Men.* New York: Reynal and Hitchcock, 1948.

Ruchames, Louis. *Race, Jobs and Politics: The Story of FEPC.* New York: Columbia University Press, 1953.

Silberman, Charles E. *Crisis in Black and White.* New York: Random House, 1965.

Spero, Sterling D., and Harris, A. L. *The Black Worker.* New York: Columbia University Press, 1931.

Stampp, Kenneth. *The Peculiar Institution.* New York: Vintage Books, 1956.

Stetler, Henry G. *Training of Negroes in the Skilled Trades.* Hartford, Conn.: Connecticut Commission on Civil Rights, 1954.

Strauss, George, and Ingerman, Sidney. "Public Policy and Discrimination in Apprenticeship," *The Hastings Law Journal,* Vol. 16, No. 3 (February 1965), pp. 285–331.

Taeuber, Irene B. *Migration, Mobility, and the Assimilation of the Negro.* Washington, D.C.: Population Reference Bureau, November 1958.

U. S. Department of Labor, Bureau of Labor Statistics. *The Economic Situation of Negroes in the United States.* Bulletin S–3, 1962.

Warren, Robert Penn. *Who Speaks for the Negro?* New York: Random House, 1966.

Washington, Booker T. "The Negro and the Labor Unions." *Atlantic Monthly* (June 1913), pp. 756–757.

Weaver, Robert C. *Negro Labor: A National Problem.* Harcourt, Brace & World, 1946.

————. "Recent Events in Negro Union Relationships," *Journal of Political Economy*, Vol. LII, No. 3 (September 1944), pp. 242–243.

Wesley, Charles Harris. *Negro Labor in the United States, 1850–1925.* New York: Vanguard Press, 1927.

Wharton, Vernon Lane. *The Negro in Mississippi, 1825–1890.* Chapel Hill: University of North Carolina Press, 1947.

Woodward, C. Vann. *The Burden of Southern History.* New York: Random House, 1961.

————. *The Strange Career of Jim Crow.* New York: Oxford University Press, 1957.

Index